THE
ELPIS
PAGES

A COLLECTIVE

EDITED BY KAYLA KING

Masthead
Kayla King, Founder, Editor-in-Chief, and Publisher
Cover art by Kayla King
Book design by Kayla King

Paperback ISBN: 9798762441780

TABLE OF CONTENTS

TABLE OF CONTENTS

But I believe she's young again
a soul immune to birthdays.
I love her here   in the desert
where new crops drink well water.

I feel how she spread her thighs
—to deliver *this*   my entire earth.

BIRTHDAY CAKES WANTED

ANISHA MANSURI

It's your Sweet 16 today but life feels sour.
You can taste the foreshadowing of change
on the tip of your tongue, watch candle flame
become nostalgia's smoke. Another piece
of cake is forced between your lips, silencing.

Slice after slice cut by your mother,
and you feel the loss as if it were your own.
Each relative taking a bite out of your insides.
Piped an icing smile upon your lips,
'Stop frowning' she says serving you a plate
'You're one step closer to becoming a woman now.'
You have no response, your mouth still full of cake.
This year has only just begun, and you feel sickly,
although maybe it's just the frosting.

It's your 18th birthday and the cake tastes
bitter-sweet, like your femininity is expiring.
Maternal eyes drag down the hem of your dress,
you look to the women who raise
the world and burn brighter than a candle flame.
For the last time, you bite your tongue
the taste of frosting tinged with copper.

21 and now the cake is gone. 21 and you decided
that you would not stop speaking, even if it made you sick.
Your words would cause them to demand cake,
just to feel sweetness again. Taste the salt, not the sugar
they were so sure you were made of. So sure you were
born with icing sugar beneath your clenched fists, although
maybe all along it was just the cake.

25 candles later and you realize
your future was never there to be reaped upon.

Not when you starred in a screenplay by the cosmos,
playing the role of a woman who freelanced as dusk
and made stars combust, all for some cake.

DIASPORA OF A HEART

LIZZIE WANN

before I knew love, I knew kindness
a shared glass of milk, empty glass left behind
because he knew I liked it

before I knew love, I knew violence
a boy at my 9th birthday party
hit me over the head with my gift –
a board game – before presenting it to me
I cried, he laughed, the other girls were jealous

before I knew love, I knew innocence
connected by a phone with no conversation
I remember his name and nothing else

before I knew love, I knew tongues
awkwardly poking each other's mouths

when I first knew love, it was true
but not meant to last

the next time I knew love, I ever so slowly mutated
became a sponge, absorbed all his likes & beliefs
but for a pinprick of light that slowly began to shine
to show me the way out

the next time I knew love, it was unrequited

the next time I was a secret

the next time was obsessive and sloppy but honest

the last time I knew love, I knew hurt & happiness
I understood that love, music, and money was not enough
that telling yourself you're choosing this is not enough

I realized our baggage is heavy
depression isn't weakness
that you can laugh together for hours
still lose yourself before you realize you're gone

love is a renewable energy
ready to be scattered again

ON DISPLAY

Rebecca is chasing fireflies
in her yard next door
when I notice her haircut.
The thin, limp length she kept
her first eight years
now swings at her shoulders
as she scampers in the dusk,
arms outstretched, fingers splayed,
hoping to catch the light and claim it.

I call her over to praise her new look
and wonder if it was
a mother's coercion
or her own idea.
I want her to know
she is beautiful
before she joins in the lifelong
worry about being pretty enough.

She smiles at my compliments
and ignores my questions
as she dances in the grass.
She only wants me to see
the green light in her fist,
now bright, now dark, now bright again
before it flies out of reach.

TREE CLIMBING

KAYLA KING

Maybe you and I might have been friends like other girls. We could keep secrets in the dark beneath stars.

Maybe.

Now is not the time.

From fog you emerge, bare-footed. You squeal at the dew chilling toes and ankles. I'd ask you to play, but I know what you would say. So, I remain quiet, settling into my place.

You must brave the wild storm of this age, always stuck between younger and older.

Your father told you this once, and he smiled when he said the words. Even now, however, the memory makes your lips pucker, as if leaving a sour taste behind. He can't understand what it means to live without a mother because his own is still alive. She lives three blocks over, and it's where you live, too.

He plans to one day claim this land, to build a home for you. Your father will call the estate Harper House. He's told you of the plan, and you've recited the recollection to me whenever it starts to rain.

I'm not sure why the change in weather brings the words easier between us, but it does, even as you try to make them disappear from your mind. You once used a twig as a magic wand, tracing it down your forehead in the hopes you could banish the things in your thoughts.

Oh, little fool, there are better ways to forget.

You hide against my limbs as if I am your mother, but I cannot hold you safe.

You always find me first.

Long ago, I might've been a mother, but I am nothing but bark and branch now. Don't search for my roots. Soon summer will make me bloom, and you can trace your small fingers over my leaves, green one way, white on the reverse; I've always been more than I seem.

When the construction on your new home begins next week, you will try to be the kind of helper you know your father would want. You will assist him in trimming me down to bare bone to be used in building a front door without ever knowing my name.

Marlowe was lost long ago. You will never find my story in the way you've discovered your mother's; she wrote her heart between the pages of a diary with delicate pages. When you read them now, you're careful not to smudge her elegant script. You try to memorize the words just in case. And every time you see your name, Margaret Harper, the feeling is tender, missing her tangible.

You might ask how I know these things, but it would be difficult to explain.

Instead, I'll let you carve your initials into my trunk. I won't force my bark back over. Instead, I will offer you leaves to frame like butterfly wings pressed edge to edge behind glass.

You can be good.

Better.

Best.

"Margaret Harper!" Your grandmother calls your name from the path. She's taken to looking for you here first on the mornings you disappear. She should understand, but she doesn't. You have the same wildness as your mother, long hair whipping free from the braid at the back of your neck.

You race to the end of the field, careful not to crush the wildflowers growing at the edge of the path. The grass is still damp. But coolness from the fog has dissipated, and already the heat from the sun has sweat prickling on your back.

"Sweetness, you forgot your lunch." Your grandmother hands you a brown paper bag without scolding.

You watched her once from my limbs, high above. You thought she might've been nice some time ago.

"And please make sure you're home before supper this time," she says.

The way her scowl settles around her lips has you promising never to be too angry.

You would hate for your face to get stuck that way, for wrinkles to edge out from all that hate. You'd rather have the small parentheses of a smile, like your mother. Sometimes you trace them over the photo you have just to remember they were real.

When your grandmother leaves, you turn back to me, running as if preparing to take off in flight. It's grand, not at all like the time you fell from my branches to the ground below. You broke your arm. You didn't visit for a month. It rained almost every day then, and I had no one to share my stories with.

I won't tell you the scary bits of my life until you're older. But even if you never hear me, sometimes it's nice to have someone here.

You leave your lunch at the base of my trunk before making the climb back to where my branches crown over the land. Now they are sharp, pointed pieces of bare bark, but soon they will be filled with those double-sided leaves you so love.

Maybe one day I will explain why it is so important to be more than you appear. But for now, maybe I shall tell you about the taste of pomegranate seeds. Maybe I'll reveal the hidden color of my human lips, how someone once called them pretty because they were stained with the juice of red fruits.

You bite into an apple before I can delve into the mythology of it all. You've read about a turtle's back being a whole world, but never have you considered the realness of beginnings. Maybe one day you will know the origins of us all, but for now the crunch of your lunch takes your mind from other things.

Sometimes I know you wish I were an apple tree instead of a white poplar. You cannot know how I've survived, and so I won't make you feel bad for wishing I was something else. People wish all the time.

I wish you were really my friend. But you are too young, and you are too human.

Though trees grow and sway and fall, they are not people either.

They cannot love.

THE BANSHEE'S SONG

VANESSA MADERER

Cousin to the siren who
Croons sweet nothings
To swindle you

The banshee instead
Mourns a haunting tune
Of only gruesome truths

Nothing unreal is used to woo;
There are no inviting scales
Nor is she cloaked in vibrant hues

One might call her song a eulogy
Which is thick, and choking too
With interwoven trills and rues

She sings of death and fear
And hate and rage and
Undeniably beautiful, her voice is, yes

But it is not the banshee who screams.
It is those who hear her.

ELEGY TO BLACKBIRDS

NATALIE MARINO

The day you die you are a mute blackbird, your wings the only things
whispering to the faraway sky. I cut August's apples into the shapes
of hearts and bake them in a tin. I eat the hearts and wait for the air
to turn amber in the autumn and then in the late afternoons I watch
the fading light dance on the pie tin I left on the shelf. The night before
I too am made a mother four and twenty of you are a harmony of dark
velvet flying out the open kitchen window as I fall asleep. I dream
of a child inside a fortune cookie holding a blank piece of paper
with a drawing instead of words—a seal smiling on the floor
and its circus trainer with fish two tiny dots lost on the horizon.

SPARROW

MOLLY GREER

I waited for you
when the snow was soft,
with little flakes tangled in my eyelashes.

I kept waiting,
even as the storm grew stronger,
and the weight of the thick snow
cemented me into a taciturn snowman:
my fingers—brittle as frozen branches,
my breath—a faint wisp of smoke from a dying fire.
And you were born late,
as expected,

and broke through my icy shell,
clawing through the frost
and chipping away at deep frostbite,
until you reached my frozen heart,
where you gently cupped it
like a fallen sparrow.

Bringing with you
the promise of a spring thaw
and mended wings.

THE ART OF MAKING EYE CONTACT

KAYLA KING

There was beauty in the savage
sectioning of pinion from wing
if only to preserve perfection

behind glass. But I won't tell you
this because your feathers take more
than one color to cloak in coal.

I'm not sure what that says about shadows,
but it must predict some profundity.
If he were with me now, he'd ask the same

riddle again and again because he understood
your flight patterns, but my obsession with the writing
desk was never quite clear. Suppose it's the way it works

with an insatiable curiosity, which I recited
before bed like a promise, never prayer.
Alas, he's not here

anymore. And now, I try not to count
your unkindness, but it's too late.
There's two of your brethren,

plus you. Together, the half of a favorite;
a token of time passing. I could break you
down and build you up in so many mythological

renderings, but maybe that's why
math never treated me right.
I was always searching for the story

in those numerals. I wander
toward the other two first, a Nordic
truth held between them like the thought

and the memory of the old gods. Should I ask
them for a sign now? Would they leave
only you? Because one must be a sure omen

of death. Though this isn't one of those dreams
where I die because I don't taste thyme. And minutes
move like any other. There is the crack

of my knee as I bend to you. I await your transition
into berserk; break of beak to the sky,
shrieks to sound like mourning songs.

I know them well, but I don't imagine them
too personally for fear I'll bring the fate
of dying upon my shoulders.

The other ravens answer from the trees,
but I pay no mind. It's the way you eat
the egg with eximious ease, which stills me

instead. I expect a splatter, but you swallow
the bright blue back like it's nothing.
I ask a question and wait for a response,

no way to know if the shape will sit in your gullet
forever. Why can't you answer?
Silence exhausts far too often

because too much has already been said.
And all at once, you resemble
my mother.

You do not speak of curses then, rubbing circles
between shoulder blades, waiting for me
to become winged and wretched

as all girls must.
You've never been one to miss
the mirage of forgetting. To think

and think without leaving a trace
of any thrasonical promises. It's not safe
to say small half-truths with blood pooling

beneath this backyard tree. We're trapped
here now. Flash of old: a father, a hammer,
quietness not unlike the sound of lying.

There's nothing subtle beyond
the front door, girls perched inside
on velvet chairs like birds in cages,

too tame to know they can leave now.
Hear them beyond the yard. Listen
to the mellifluous meter of meaning mouthed

into the matted grass below. Do not pretend
to portend anything past this nothing
and nothing. We were once young, too.

It's how this should end, but it won't.
This is not our place to tell these girls
of realness, and they'll find lips to bite,

other birds to make them
believe they might one day
be mothers.

FOR YOU. MY SISTER

TESSA SWACKHAMMER

two sparrows, from the same old oak tree
born with wings made of silver and crooked feet
telling each other stories
that taste like clouds and galaxies
telling each other they'd be together
no matter the paths they lead

dancing, dancing, dancing,
        into the stars and into their dreams
        for a second, forgetting the brimstone
        and burning in their beaks

saying, sister, I am here,
and I will keep you safe
saying, sister, I am here,
and
    we will catch that break
saying, sister, I am here,
   and everything is okay

when our wings, too heavy and shoulders, too weak
when we turn to the future and the future seems bleak,
yes, even then—we will
        raise our bird necks, refuse
        and believe, and believe until we are free

o sweet sparrow now,
bow your head
and tilt your crown,
I am here, and you are never alone

together we will fly;
crawl, walk, whimper
and bring ourselves home.

MY SISTER: A FORGOTTEN DAUGHTER OF THE ISLAND

AISHWARYA KHALE

On the day of my sister's funeral, the clouds thundered over our paltry Island. It was the midsummer of May 1972. Heat rippled and parrots screamed out of the Peepul beneath a glaring, pewter sky. Thunder rumbled, announcing an impending storm on the horizon.

Maa, Baba, and I huddled together in a shed as the storm passed away. We watched the pyre grow, blazing into a fire mountain, cascading, backed against the violent sea. The tempest's wind couldn't topple it over.

Even in her death, my sister burned bright.

The pyre fizzled as twilight loomed around us. We didn't take our eyes off the sea until the fire went out, ashes scattered to the waves.

* * *

It was two weeks and five days after her death when the realization settled on us. I'd left the tap open, and it flooded the living room. I scrambled to remember. How had I forgotten to turn it off? Again. Maa and Baba realized much later.

When the mourning guests visited us, I'd sit in a corner, and ask them why they were here. I would forget to have dinner, only to eat twice in the middle of the night and vomit it. I would delete my sister's pictures and then search for them frantically in my phone. Maa would cry and scream, "I do not want any of this." They watched their two daughters evaporate, slowly and then sharply, then all of a sudden, unlearning their own rules. The boats lost their oars and the lighthouse stopped navigating ships.

The doctor's report from the city arrived on the Sunday ship. Amnesia. An aftermath of grief. My sister's parting gift.

* * *

The island of port Port Adamaro was a scattered affair with the port at one end, the old factory at the other. In between the two, dwelled a town which had no desire to thrive.

Our Island had small colonies and a quaint quality that did not seem to grow on you right away. The days were the same, like the Mandavi over the harbor flowing so slow into the island, one couldn't see it.

It all began with the murmurs and whispers. On the day of the funeral, the members from the opposition party came by in their jeeps, flaring their party's flag. They had put up hoardings and graffities all over the Island.

Long live the purity…

The Panthers are an American menace. We do not want them on our soil too. They circled in the city market with loudspeakers.

The Dalits from the neighboring town had attended her funeral. Police intervened only to let the killers go off on bail. Floating in the middle of the sea, our island was not safe. The violence had seeped onto our little Island. Distance couldn't really hide the human ugliness.

Our Island had flourished when my sister lived, now bleeding with musky tears of brown soil streams. On Sundays, we would go down to the beach. Maa, Baba, Sister and I would go to the market and buy snacks. We would carry a picnic basket and would fish by the harbor. Sister and I would sleep on Maa's lap and Baba would tell us stories.

My sister had become a ghost. An imaginary figment of our memory.

I would forget to carry books to school, the word for stairs became the word for sky and the curry cooking on the pan would dry into a thick paste. I would stack random items together: common juice boxes, caps, books, underwear, pencil shavings, wax cream.

I found myself forgetting conversations, discussing fuddled foggy memories, repeating stories over again, and cherishing strangers as old friends. My mind felt like a pulp mango, ripe with the memories of my past, but slowly sulking and rotting into a yellow lifeless seed.

The report revealed numerous spikes. A zig zag of green and blue lines. A terrain of my diseased brain. I forgot what my sister looked like. She faded away from the puzzle of my mind, one piece at a time, rumbling and smashing into the other pieces. Trying to make up an image

48

that no longer existed. To make up something that had already been forgotten.

The local doctor analyzed the report. He sat down beside me, with a notepad in his hand, and looked at me with a countenance of utter vulnerability. "You will forget", he said. I wasn't upset at the sheer notion of my sister's absence. I was forgetting, while the others had already forgotten. Who would remind them?

"It is an incurable disease."

It was not a disease; it was how humans survived.

We forget. We do not want to remember the things that make us uncomfortable. Baba, Maa, the trees, the sand, the sun, everyone had let go. I wouldn't.

It was during the morning prayer that I'd questioned my sister. She had peddled on the cycle, back to the house in the wee hours of the morning. She had escaped through the back door and came home with a document hidden beneath the pleats of her saree.

"Don't tell Baba", she said. I nodded. It was then, the beginning of the end.

* * *

Baba had been to the city. When he came back, he announced that I would be going to a college in the city. Maa was apprehensive. Sister was elated.

"Why don't you come with me?" I asked her.

"To babysit you?" She laughed, "No, please".

"What do you want? You could teach in a school or a college."

"From you? Or life?"

"What do you want for yourself?" She had looked out of the window.

"You'll come visit me?" She promised.

We loitered at the park, eating coconut ice cream to celebrate. Sister saw a Nightingale sitting on the tree. She stared at him for far too long. It was a few minutes before I realized that she was stuck. I waited for a long time. I was looking at her and she did not seem like herself.

Sister picked out the key with yellowed fingers, "How many nights?" She shrugged and continued to speak with the man. His silhouette was stiff, like spare people whom no one is concerned to introduce. I was now an accomplice in her late-night charades. We'd cross the narrow road between the high ivied walls that ran along the creek behind the parallel side of the ruined old factory. There, a man would collect the papers and the leaflets. He did not dare to count or read the text. He patted her with respect.

That is some good work comrade," the man said.

At the time, I believed she was meeting boyfriends. The man then left the ruins, looking around to make sure he was not followed. Not that there was anyone to follow him, but it was a sound procedure. We entered our backyard by the iron gate, climbing up the tree, and skirting across the roof to our bedroom window.

On other days when the house seemed silent, when Maa and Baba had an early dinner, she would slip into the bleak dark of the night and disappear into the obscure madness, to come home at dawn with the nocturnal wind. She would stretch into her bed, smiling at me through the sheets to wake up with a fiery expedition at the first drop of Baba's morning call.

* * *

In my own lifetime, the creek had changed from blue to dead grey-brown, so thickened with the scum that humans bring with them, that seeing one's feet in the shallows was impossible.

Sister persuaded me to come for the poetry reading event at the school. She was a teacher at the only school on the Island. The kids wrote about local folklores and mythical monologues. Only the Dalits, one kid recited, are brought together by forces unknown, so very far from the many rivers and the roads and are deserted into tiny islands and secluded waters across India. The other recited a poem: *The golden nightingale of the empire wails, who has withdrawn sailing earthward. One could glimpse her shadow against the edge of the moon, disappearing from the daylight.*

* * *

In the sun and silence, I would sit on the warm trunk of a fallen Peepal tree, from where one could see the old post office. Perhaps before, the goons had marched there with their guns and batons, finding my sister's post records. They had ransacked the office, leaving letters and documents flying through the roof, stomping over them, frantically looking for any evidence.

It was the first incident. December 1971.

The goons from the opposition party, who led the anti-Dalit rally, had received an anonymous tip that had every postal detail coming to the Island. In the quiet that followed, they traced links coming from international cargoes- The clippings of the Panther Chronicle, letters to the Panthers, leaflets, post from the Americans. The letters which started with: *My brothers and my sisters.*

I knew then that the world was constructed solely for subjugation, nothing was fair, and forgetting was necessary. I still feel how wrong I was then. They cajoled Maa and Baba. They ransacked our home. We had our mouths half open, breathing slowly, eyes suspended over the batons. One of them spoke to Baba; it was a small husky sound, barely a whisper but clean and distinct: She stops, or we kill her.

* * *

I focus, steadily, on a moment from my own past. I have watched my mind evaporate like camphor into the air, in love with what is left of my sister. On Fridays, I practice remembering her voice, duplicating her walk, mimicking her body language, humming songs the way she would to which my Maa interrupts me, "Stop, you won't remember!".

At night, when Baba falls asleep, I hug Maa, pressing my face into her chest, and listening to her heartbeat while whispering sighs of grief. We both shut our eyes and endure through the night.

I dance to music to realize that I have been listening to the same song for half an hour. I keep waking up in the middle of the night and walk towards the window. Peering into the dim shade of the abyss at the end of the street, I expect Sister to wave at me, promising she'll be home soon. I wake up in the morning, and the rest of the night seems like a blur.

51

Amnesia and grief are sisters; they work hand in hand.

My mind is persistent; it doesn't remember. I try to keep a last broken picture of my sister in my mind, but it holds on to its desire to burn it away.

The neighbors come by to ask for some salt and sugar. It frightens me, Maa and Baba have forgotten. The days refuse to change in her absence. I cannot tell if she was here. Her ghost lingers somewhere. But not here.

Once in a while, when I am in my bed, not asleep, I see Maa and Baba standing in the doorway of my bedroom watching me. I know their thoughts. They think of my sister and how they cannot keep me away from harm. There is no answer, but they are relieved that I am forgetting. I could see the dissatisfaction and the jealousy their eyes screamed; like they were the ones who deserved to forget it more than I did.

* * *

The doctor switches off the machine and scribbles on his pad. *July 1973- Visible positive symptoms.* How do I tell him I need medicines before I forget her or a reminiscing syrup for Maa and Baba? It frightens me, the lingering silence, and the comfortable oblivion that everyone has settled into. In forgetting her, we are erasing a part of who we are.

I look out of the hospital window, and I see fleeting images; I envisage faces peering through the sails, searching for the forgotten voice that had chanted from a tiny island and echoed across oceans and continents.

My mind struggles to keep her alive. I panic; will I forget her? Perhaps in the end, I will not remember her at all. Perhaps, she will be forgotten. The doctor prescribed me the medicine. The report says positive. "It is not forgetting, but remembering that we need," I murmur. The doctor does not hear me. I want to scream instead.

On weekends Baba and I play songs on my sister's piano. In the late evening we visit the department store. I buy biscuits for us to eat by the beach. Maa scuffles around in the food section. There are many tourists buying fishing supplies in the store. The beach is crowded and there are youngsters buying alcohol from the store. Baba waits by the door for us.

Mine is a family of believers. There are lies which are fading away and diminishing with time. We either deem to accept it or forget it. But the Island remembers.

The collective amnesia basks on the surface, till it chips into tiny screams which seep into the Island, deeper and stronger by night. The Island shakes at the nonchalant animosity and the sheltering of the forgotten. It births baby turtles and baby crabs between the same sand grains.

Only the Island remembers. It rumbles in her memory. The coconuts crack open, and the leaves recite her tales. The baby turtles grow older and ask their mothers about my sister. The ocean growls and the Peepul's roots reach for the soil wanting to go back into the earth. The Island slips into the rhythm and its shadow strangles me. The Island howls for her.

I glance out the window. It begins to drizzle. People run to get shelter. I look at Maa and she smiles at me through the shelves. Outside a storm thunders and the Island, it roars.

MARY AND ROSE

EILEEN EARHART OLDAG

It is August or worse in Kosciusko.
Rose is dead
and gray as the unpainted porch
where Alex cuts her box through flies and sweat,
another daughter gone.
Mary sways at her sister's left side
eye on the white gown

cotton and pleats
that gives illusion of wedding.
Ear to the women kneeling around the board, crying
"Who can save us? This girl
is dead as she became a woman.
Her blood went wrong,
came up instead of down.
Confirmed in ritual and white one day,
coughed blood the next.
Not even God can save if you are woman."

On the hard stone above her head,
Lucifer's split toe taps.
"Rise, Rose. I will have you for a bride."
She nods, shakes loose her braid and takes his hand.
They dance like moonlight
on barn roof and windowsill.

Like moonlight they dance on cedar branch
and dance again in Mary's yellow eye
as she tells how they stopped on the unrailed bridge
leaned to watch the creek
cut its coffin in sandstone,
how Rose fell
and shattered on the water
her dress a thousand shards of moonlight in the current,

and Lucifer helpless because
the devil cannot save if you are woman.

Somewhere between an empty heaven and August in Kosciusko
Mary sits at a window praying to no one
for Rose's return.
Every other fortnight her vigil is rewarded
when a round, puzzled moon rises,
pieced together from shallow runs,
an unsaved sister, dancing and dying.

ELEGY FOR THE REMAINING
ONE

MELODY WANG

somber eyes of amber cast downward
over the dark depths of the sea, you emerged
from a time of old when the murmurs of ancient elms
transcended the drones of man and drifted softly
only to settle into the lulling waves

when silent symphonies of twilight
cascade around you, you close your eyes
of flame and sorrow as your spilled life—
blood turns into mist and hovers around your head
as a fragile glistening web of the finest silver

you reach out a trembling hand
as if to either coax back this lattice
untainted by the darkest of storms
or to push away the very essence
that has sustained your life for so long

in that moment, the whole universe pulsates
with all the forces of darkness and light,
with secrets whispered but never discerned
by men. You exhale and droplets cascade down
your hair, effulgent perhaps for the last time

all is still now, aside from the waves that gently
caress your cold corpse as it quickly turns pale
with a growing cavity where rivulets of radiance
once coursed through—on your face: the faintest
smile echoes secrets that fade into luminescence

HALF A LOAF

MARGARET KOGER

Summers versed in sunshine
Hot rhymes splashed on soaked skin
Rafting a wet, downriver line

Bees drinking from nectarines
Humming their plainsong airs
Sticky legs clad in pollen dispatch

Fertile as we could have been
If I'd known the danger of flat notes
Messing with harmony

Paying tribute to mixed messages
A scree of slippery sentence fragments
Lips stunned by fractured kisses

Lips failing to find words
Curses stashed in high cupboards
Swarming in empty vases

Words unheard in ticking rhythms
To work, to school, to listen for news
Not of our making

Even in September a ray of sun
Like a pot of syrup under a maple tree
A dandelion surprise

Smiling as I once was dressed
In a satin wedding gown, you in a tux
White cake frippery

But harvesting no sugar plums
I swayed like a tree bent by the wind
Leaves falling in refrains

Stanzas written in bursts of stormy
Tears sweating the yeast in a bread dough
Brewing until the loaf is baked.

"Half a Loaf" - John Heywood's 1546 glossary *A dialogue conteinyng the nomber in effect of all the prouerbes in the englishe tongue*: Throwe no gyft agayne at the giuers head, / For better is halfe a lofe then no bread.

IN CLASS, THE FILM BUFFERS
AS ICARUS DIES

KYRAH GOMES

The day is indifferent to my survival.
Clouds don't cease their strange shapes
when I paste my eyelids shut. I've watched
Icarus 'plummet hundreds of times, the image
of his exhilaration singed into my retinas.
I inhabit metaphors which grow inside of me,
parasitic. Putting out unwelcome roots,
trying to split concrete slabs. Pity me,
my worn out muse, the mindless burning.
Someday, this tired spectacle will fossilize.
All along, the thing in the burning book was me.

THE WRIT OF THE DAY

MANJUSHA HARI

Burst,
Burst the rapturous sorcery of my scents
and let me see your rapt face,
as the secret of an autumn glow.
Let the fleeting pleasures define us!

Derive me,
by sifting the poetry from you
and let your wriggles speak!
The yearn for darkness,
the stained valance,
The obdurate time,
the immolated shyness.
The redeemed self of my ardent, woeful desires,
may rewrite you as the verse of a nightmare!
Let it be!
The selfishness of my lost verve
and madness
blazing by reflecting you!
I'm cursing this delusive reality,
too lost in an insane, profound dream!

SUMMER APPLES

MARGARET KOGER

The power of spring sunlight
warmed the lips of twigs,
formed buds   unfolded blossoms
itching for bees to spread gold lamé
on their stigmas   pollen carrying
sperm down tubes   to ovules
as in so many female buds.

Surrounded by sheltering leaves
ripened apples invite our teeth
to bite into their crisp flesh
a tart dance on the tongue.

Summer apples meant to replace
barrels of root cellar has-beens,
only not quite   because the new girls
arrived before the berries were done.

We pick a few   bake pies   leave
the rest to tumble into weeds where
they'll be gathered to feed the hogs.

Some year there'll be a free-for-all
boys flinging their ardent desires at
side-stepping girls   or so I imagine.

I see the hogs   the trees   and me
as if I too were a giggly dancer
dodging apples   hoping a suitor
will come to court me   or else
the fruits of my body may be lost
left to rot   to brown in the sun
bees drunk on abandoned sugars.

APPLE ORCHARD

ANAUM

We were in an apple orchard
He was sitting beside me
And had held my hand
He had interlocked his fingers within mine as he spoke of the times ahead
As he spoke those words, it felt he was narrating something he had already experienced
As if he had known of those moments in his dreams
and was planning to live them now
Honestly, I was distracted
I was worried that my father would be coming from mosque
We looked at stars
He whispered in my ear the names he had thought of our children
And I had blushed
We were fifteen and were under the blanket of stars and roof of apple trees
In moments of crimson abyss
He was speaking of dreamed times as
I had felt him tumbling upon my shoulder
His head had dropped down
I thought he was trifling around
Then
What I heard was bang of door
Father must have come home
It was a doomed thought that overwhelmed my mind
I ran without looking back at him
I went inside
As if protecting my hymen
Yet I felt wetness upon my shoulder
Light was dim
But not so dim to hide glare of his blood on my shoulder
Upon my hands
I apprehended something,
and it punched me out of my senses

I ran out like a woman who had lost her husband
Praying I really wouldn't end that way
There I saw men shouldering coffin
Coffin of somebody I hadn't looked back at in his moments of death
He was shot in head with gun in hands of someone too good at his trade
His craft had silenced silence
Fifteen years have passed now
They say I am a married woman now
Father had told me his name, but I wasn't a traitor
Who would trade his country twice
I aborted twice
I had to send my children to their young teen father.

MALE-FEAR / MENARCHE

CHRISTINE NAPRAVA

I rated you a ten and you stuck me with a seven,
which on that night in that living room with those girls

felt like a horse kick to a gut that wasn't mine.
Those were the beginning days,

front-camera photographs taken,
and front-camera photographs heavily edited,

and front-camera photographs uploaded for others.
On my Facebook wall, I was a solid eight,

a you're-really-pretty-we-should-get-to-know-each-other eight,
only I never got to know them, and I don't know myself, still.

In the shadow of that seven,
you asked me how far I'd been with a guy

and then you invited me to an Uncle Kracker concert,
twenty eleven, freshman year.
I couldn't think of anything worse—

I thought of us alone in a baseball-capped, flannel-shirt-clad crowd,
a side hug turned front hug turned tongue-far-down-throat hug–

but I insisted on a wishy-washy maybe because at that time,
I was fourteen and just learning
to keep a dozen condemned doors open.

I blew you off.

Then my male-fear set in,
two thousand three, a roundup of registered sex offenders

plastered on the local newspaper's front page,
Mother's half-ass reassurance (*they can't get you*),

and with your pubescent senses pricked,
you came looking for me at my family's yard sale,

pumping circles in my driveway as your best friend wondered
where my friend was but which one, which friend.

I had so many and now I have none.
My mother lied for me. She's not home.

We never even kissed.
I hadn't had my first kiss yet.

You had a year on me,
that's it, that's all, a few months, trivial.

I can't remember your birthday.
Perhaps if I knew your zodiac,

it'd explain why I projected years of
deep-seated male-fear onto your barely teenage body.

You live in Florida now.
Your name is too generic to yield a gratifying Google search.

You are forever shaggy blond and heavy cheek acne,
my only blond, a real-life Kurt Cobain,

although Kurt had a jawline when he died
and yours hadn't had time to develop yet.

I cannot separate you from the horror of my first period,
the salmon-pink discovery,

the gym class bounce house that followed,
even though on that day of fated bloodshed,

I didn't know you yet.

WILD GIRLS

CLAIRE TAYLOR

after Mary Oliver

You were told to be good
to not drop to your knees
for any man who didn't walk a hundred miles through the desert,
not let your body, soft and animal
         surrender to love.
Tell me about your desires, and I'll tell you mine.
Meanwhile the world—
scorching sun and pelting rain
across abandoned landscapes—cuts rivers
through the prairie of your memory, roots deep.
Meanwhile wild geese, high in the air,
are free to head home again.
Wherever you are, no matter how lonely,
the world offers little consolation.
These wild girls, harsh and exciting—
calling out over and over. There's no place for you
in this family anymore.

FAKE IT TIL YOU MAKE IT

ELYSSA TAPPERO

they say "fake it 'til you make it"
so here I am, a child playing dress-up
wearing my mother Bast's smile and poise
Inanna's confidence and Hathor's positivity
and the Morrigan's steel spine underneath it all

if I walk like them, talk like them
will I be strong like them?
will I be brave like them?
will I be good like them?

FOR MY FAIR MAIDENS,

AI JIANG

Look. No, not at the fair- haired maiden
sitting by the mirror, holding up lipstick—
it is only a pose, an unreal picture. No,
not the half-naked girl whose pictures
you took and placed on the nightstand
with photos of fairy tales and princesses.
You know you will never achieve
such idealism, such beauty, such glory
that floats you above clouds and crowns
you in gold rays of sunshine only
to disappear when you look in the mirror.

Look. Yes, you are that fair maiden
staring at your phone screen. No,
not the photoshopped image you cropped
so your limbs look less gnarly. No,
not the one you twisted, you bent,
you smeared away the blemishes
and imperfections until you look nothing
like yourself. You turned on max the Contrast
and Highlight and Brightness and Saturation.
There is no crown when you can't see
above your head or even the left side
of your face because you think
the right side is your only good side.

Look. No, not at the camera. Look. No,
not at the mirror. Look. Yes, on the inside.
Because that is all you need to feel.

TO STAVE OFF MY
IMPENDING MEMORY LOSS

MELODY WANG

these days, I document it all: equations,
        too-long lists of groceries and feelings,
                books and songs I promise my friends

I'll check out, but never quite seem
        to get around to. Haiku sequences
                of my nightly dreams, laden with those

sticky images of my unprocessed
        childhood traumas: sterile hallways
                with that nasty fluorescent green

glow to highlight this swelling lump
        of unease when I straddle the lucid
                states of being and unbeing. I awaken

gasping in the gloom of a waning moon.
        I long to grasp some familiar outstretched
                hand, palm steady in the gloaming: see

how my own limbs unfurl to draw close
        to the warmth I have for too long denied
                myself, seemingly just out of reach, as if

in a dream: a softly murmured mantra
        mists down upon me like an anointing.
                For once, I allow myself the space to be.

WOMANHOOD IN MEASURES

CHRISTIANA JASUTAN

I spread my arms so they see me
doesn't matter   a tree or a   woman
both they will cut up
touch me   as if I'm a sapling   forever green
at the tips of my words   milk me dry   drink my sap
drink me   render me rubber   thank me
take the children at my feet   take them
as donations   as sachets of fresh blood
someone in a blood bank always thinks they never sacrifice enough

ENOUGH

ELLEN CLAYTON

To be a woman
is to believe you are
too much
yet simultaneously
not enough.
The skin you are in
is never sufficiently smooth,
your body never the right
size or shape.
Shrink, shrink,
keep shrinking
until you barely
inhabit
space.
Be quiet:
your voice is
excessively loud.
You are not funny.
You're too opinionated.

That is what they say.
Fuck them all.

You will never win so
Quit
the game.
Stop apologizing for
existing.
Walk into a room
as if you fucking own it,
chest proud,
head high—
Take   up   space

Let truth spill from your
lips in a torrent:
emphatic.
Your body is not
a trophy or painting
It is your vessel
and you are the sole captain.
Treat yourself with respect
and kindness.
Go forth and give this world
what it needs:
all of you
Unapologetically.

ADULTHOOD IS A VIOLENT THING

CHRISTIANA JASUTAN

like that red gash
on your torn paper-thin lips.
Your body ejaculates excess hemoglobin
from your private parts.
(What private parts?)

Blood is just different shades of the sky:
dusk-dark, half twilight and night
dawn-dipping orange gushing red.
(Does the sky always splatter?)

Red mist on your underwear
the earliest sign of life wiped vigorously
with tissue paper, you wash and wash and wash
until your knuckles split and it smells rancid
underwater.
(Why does it not smell like life?)

You've never seen life curdle
like strawberry milk.
If you scrape deep enough
there is always a pomegranate seed.
Our bodies are mere husks.
*(Is it a part of me that is a shell for another human
or is it the entirety of me?)*

PRELUDE

CAROLJEAN GAVIN

I am sloshing through the blood
And lipstick and juice
Of my womanhood
In new red spike high-heeled shoes
Screaming.

The devil's in my eyes.
I know.
And in my toenails.
In my fiery hair,
Thar flares and flames and rages
From my head.
From my bed.
The devil's in there too.
I know.

And it's ok.

The devil's in my red sports car.
Murderous sports car.
And we're painting the town red.

I never saw when my mother bled.
But she must have.
She must have.

I kicked myself out,
Raw, screaming,
Blood curdling,
Congealing.

Honey, you're sweeter than
Raspberry syrup,

Raspberry syrup
Whirled and twirled on my china plate.

Fasting on cherries and Chinese food
Wine flows thick.
With obsidian teeth, I draw another draught.
Drunk on who I am
And who I've been.
I want to spit the taste of woman out.
I swallow and swallow and
Swallow and
Swallow.

And my red sports car swallows the road.
The devil is giggling behind a lipsticked smile.
I thrust my red shoe down harder for the next mile.
I could drive like this forever.
People becoming streaks, boring little streaks of mundane color,
Memories livid little streaks like blood and murder.
Streaking past streaks, street after street
I feel fine.

Red wine
Drips
From your wrists and
Ankles,
I part my lips and
Draw my searing tongue to lick.

Passion's devil.
My little sequined shimmy and hip sway.
Flashing red lights are beautiful at night.
We'll dance to the street's siren and I don't even
Need to know your name.
You gave me a rose.
A red, red, red rose,
And I love you
Even though I'm bleeding.

Thorns thrust,
Plunged into my heart,
Beating and trying to recover,
So I can devour

Every last trace of you.
Every last trace of dying and trying to be a woman
That I'm not.
Trying to be what they told me I was.
Trying to deny everything I am.
Trying to deny my blood,
My thighs, my pretty little head.
My pretty little head
Wishes you were dead
A gory little pool at the bottom of a wishing well.
I do wish you well.

The devil's in my red sports car,
Murderous sports car.
A kiss from lipsticked lip
To lipsticked lip, we say farewell.
I slide out of the car and back into hell.

SANCTUARY

STEPHANIE PARENT

In the little log cabin
Deep in the womb of the woods
With the seven little men who were not men
She was safe

She thought she was safe
When the little men left
For the mines, to unearth
Their precious jewels—

After all, the sun was shining
The fire popped and crackled in the hearth
She'd scrubbed the cooking pot till it gleamed
And swept all the dirt from the floor
And outside the clothes on the line fluttered
Like happy ghosts in the breeze
While the bunnies white as dandelion puffs
Hopped beneath

All that work, an offering
What could she hope for, in return?

The dwarves would be home before dark
Just enough time
For the old woman
To place her paper hand
On the fence's gate
To set down her basket of wares and
Look right at Snow
With a smile that could melt

Just enough time
For the woman to lace Snow's bodice

With ribbons the color of blood, of lips, of roses
Her paper hands still trembling
Till that last moment when she pulled tight—

Snow didn't notice
She was looking for something
In the old woman's eyes
And trying to decide
Whether they were brown or blue

The dwarves came home just as the last breath
Was escaping Snow's red lips
The bunnies had retreated to their burrows
The birds had ceased their song

But Snow's hope did not escape

The next morning, the dwarves left again
And Snow wondered if another
Kinder visitor might arrive

She did—
Another old woman
With eyes the soft blue of the stream
That meandered just outside the cabin
How could such a woman
Bring anything but soft, sweet life?

She offered Snow a comb
Clutched in her spun-wool hands
Snow hoped for the feeling of those fingers
Stroking her hair softly
Lovingly

She got the poison comb instead

That night, the dwarves revived her
The bunnies looked on with button eyes
Snow gazed beyond the gate and saw
The dark edge of danger in the sky

But in the morning, the sun was butter
Melting all the gloom

So when the third old woman came
With eyes the brown of wise tree trunks
That have stood tall and offered
Shelter and shade
Snow took the apple from that whorled wood hand
Without a thought
She bit into the woman's gift, her love
To take it inside herself

Even as she tasted the bitter beneath the sweet
Snow knew, she knew, she knew

THE IMPLICATIONS OF LIPSTICK

JULIA FIGLIOTTI

I want to look
                    pretty
          but not
                    too pretty

I want to look
                    good
          but not
          so good
that someone else decides
                    he has a right
          to touch
          to taste
          to keep trying after I say
(however I say)
                    No.

I want to love my body
          but not
                    so much
          that society and a court of law find me
                              Guilty
          for someone else's entitlement
to love it for me

          my body
          my choices
          his choices
          his actions
all under my control

                    until he leaves something behind

then "my choices"
(in which I had no say)
            leave me with no choice
            but to carry the weight of
                        his choices
                        his actions
                                    which I was responsible for
                                    because
I wanted to look
                        pretty

THE MORNING BEFORE PILL

ABBIE MADIGAN

I sat down for the interview and it started with the frequent use of verbs and nouns and those actions that the old drunks use on a Saturday when they want to grab hold of that young girl and choke her in a back alley and watch the cosmos erupt behind her closed eyes and she fights it and slumps forward.

Follow the variety of meanings and applications and just watch that cosmos erupt when the door opens and we just scream "sit" at those plastics and she coos hello to the old women and she falls over and drops her umbrella and watch that cosmos erupt behind her eyes.

She stumbled and let the actions of yesterday become cardigan notions of what she felt when she picked up that phone and let the receiver answer the laptop because technology just wants to talk to itself.

Those old men just sipped their beer and laughed at her falling and picking up glass just trying to find her reflection in the mirror and then the interviewer asked me which applejack I wanted, and I just whimpered and monotone my response that I just needed to let the scarecrow jack straw leave me be for ten minutes.

But the words just split from his mouth about picking left over right and why do I like green and what's wrong with purple and I interweaved it all just as the cosmos erupted behind my eyes and I just grabbed hold of the edge of the bed, and she let her fingers trace the stars alignment.

I licked up obediently all the colors between green and purple and then just let his vuvuzela flow and let it all dissipate into a sign - she whimpered, and they just picked her up and tossed her into a bin where she became a little lost and Terry has a wife did you know? Every night he goes home and traces her back to that sweet milky way and every morning he likes to take a piece out that tossed up bin and just let her fly and fly and—

82

"Are you sure you wanted to answer that?" The interviewer touched my knee, and I didn't shudder or shiver I just let the touch of skin-on-skin blemish me and then pass over and if I look out of the window will I manage to get here to there or just be lost in a constant straight road of nowhere?

Then he opened the door and the cosmos erupted behind my eyes as she slipped like an eel from a womb or the bin and crawled across the street and bumped into a lamppost with the left side of her frontal lobe and she just let out more than a sigh and and and when that lamppost hit the cosmos erupted behind her eyes.

Terry lifted up the bin and pulled out an apple core that had become rotten overnight like a perfect bright berried white light and he took a bite and as he chewed the old men filled up their beers took a sip and I watched them and when I walked over and told them what they did to that girl with the lamppost that night they let out a sigh and I produced those pictures from that day and they said it was their bodies in the picture yes but not their minds.

CAT CALLS

ELYSSA TAPPERO

You see only a soft housecat;
you forget I've yet my claws and teeth.

If you hurt me I will bite.
If you hurt me I will scratch.
If you hurt me I will hurt you worse
and your wounds will fester and weep.

You see only a soft housecat;
you forget I'm yet a beast.

CLAWS

HOLLEY LONG

I dream of fingers
turning into claws,
blades punching through the
skin between knuckles.
Delicate hands or deadly weapons:
a gentle caress or a crushing blow.
But that power belongs to comic pages, so I
slip keys between my fingers,
and I make due.
Clacking heels echoing on concrete:
a death march.
Cavernous space swallows each step.
I am here, I am here, they announce.
Head on a swivel, eyes always roving.
Elbows tuck in with locked energy—
a necessary posture.
Friendly words may precede offense.
So a smile becomes a defense.
Teeth grit against unspoken pleas.
Hoping. Praying. This is it.
Please let that be it.
Ears train on receding steps, listen for a halt—
fingers squeeze, keychains bite into soft skin.
Predators can prowl
but I am not prey.
Car beeps.
I look for reflections in the windows,
see only my face
beneath a mask of practiced stone.
Grip the handle, slip inside a fortress, locks snap back in place.
Breathe. Breathe.
I'm going
home.

THE GIRL WITH THE PEARL EARRING

JASMINA KUENZLI

The girl with the pearl earring never said a word. She didn't speak. There were men and women talking over her head, like she was a child at the dinner table.

In the painting, she looks over her shoulder at the artist, but there is not kindness behind her eyes. No inquisitiveness or calm, or even love. There is the edge of fear. The hint of disobedience.

The girl with the pearl earring is wearing clothes that don't belong to her in a house that she only works in and somehow, everything is still her fault. The girl with the pearl earring is a story of harassment, of beauty as a curse. She has big, beautiful eyes and soft, moist lips, and when she looks at you, you kind of *stop*. The light hits her face just the way you want it to, the way you dreamed it.

The girl with the pearl earring is a stroke of inspiration.

So you use her. You sit her atop a stool, and you have her mix in the colors for her eyes and unbind her hair, and even when she asks you not to look, you press. Even when she turns away, you still stare. You play with the laces of your shirt and wonder about the girl with the pearl earring that you stole for, who hardly says a word, who barely strings a sentence together. The girl who never smiles, but whose eyes are pleading when you ask her to stand in front of you again.

Let the light hit her. Drive the needle through her ear, let her blood stain your wife's pearls, and get drunk on the wine. Your friend is in the other room listening for the sound of the girl with the pearl earring. In the courtyard, he'll corner her like she's an animal, and she won't say a word, not even *no*, not even *stop*, because she's just the girl with the pearl earring, and she's not where she's supposed to be even when she's following directions.

You hold her entire life in your hands with the same marked indifference as you do the canvas where you mix your paints. She is a surface for your vision. What do you care if she never sees the butcher's boy? What do you see of the marks on the side of her neck?

The girl with the pearl earring is dismissed, summarily, once you have painted your vision. You don't need the flesh and blood anymore—she is encased in the frame, and her eyes are still boring into you with just a hint of accusation. When you look at her, you can't help but think of the way she looked when your wife slapped her across the face. She was only an object, only a thing to be gazed upon. She is just the girl with the pearl earring, and it's all her fault.

You send her a message sealed in your paint with the pearl earrings encased, but her ear is swelling from the infection, and the butcher's boy thinks she slept with you because if you had asked, she would have had to, because she is just the girl with the pearl earring, and the butcher's boy knows that it means she is nothing but a figure encased in paint and immortalized in convenience, forever.

The girl with the pearl earring is remembered outside of your name, in the recommendations of boys to pretty girls with delicate headbands, in office buildings and conference rooms where the girl steps around the men talking carefully, desperate to be the person in the room who doesn't have to stand and be gazed upon, who can take it and hold it like power between her fingers, like the keys she holds out to catch someone who gets too close.

The girl with the pearl earring has a name. And at night, she imagines holding someone's hands in the dark, with none of those gazes peering out her from between the walls and through the window. The girl with the pearl earring still doesn't have a single thing to call her own, but her hair is worn down sometimes, in all its snarling glory, and she holds her head high and keeps her eyes up, and when she gets a compliment, she doesn't swallow it, or proclaim false modesty.

And the girl with the pearl earring scratches at her painting every day and lets it flake away, and you shout that she is destroying the masterpiece, that time is rendering her image mutable and ever changing, that if it disappears, she will, too.

But the girl with the pearl earring exists in other places than the inside of your mind. And even as the chill runs up your spine, you can feel the color blossom into her skin, her eyes brighten, her hair cascade.

And as you crumble to ash, flaking away bit by bit with every century, and every footstep, and every comment that she no longer demurs, flutters her eyelashes at, or sweeps aside…

She picks up a brush and begins to create.

NORMAL PROBLEMS

PAM R. JOHNSON DAVIS

How wonderful it is to have normal problems.
I never had them before.
I was so busy waiting for the next blow to knock me off my feet
Or fearing the feel of unwanted hands
To be concerned by the air conditioning going out
Or a flat tire
Or the Wi-Fi speed

You see, there was no room for normal problems.
I was busy being Black and woman
Worried that I might pose a threat
So I made myself softer, more presentable
to the palettes of those who would cause me harm

I never had time for normal problems like slow moving traffic
Or rains that flood the garden a little
Because the foundation on which I built my life was sinking
Cracked from years of covering up what went down
To protect everyone around me from knowing
there was a predator in our midst

So I never saw normal problems like the movie theater
being out of my favorite popcorn mix
Or speeding tickets
Or the line for my favorite drive thru being long.
I was too busy counting down how much longer
I had to be away from the pain that awaited me.

I couldn't be bothered by normal problems.
I was so busy trying to heal
That I didn't have time for pollen-induced allergies
Or irritated skin
I was too busy trying to mask myself, my body from prying eyes
so that they would not see

the real me

I couldn't make space for normal problems because I was busy
piecing myself together after being lost for so long
Haunted by the memories, unable to sleep without the lights on

So you see, how wonderful it is for me to have normal problems
Like arguing about the placement of the couch in our living room,
both of us with ideas about how to maximize the space around us
only to collapse together on the couch to make memories of our love

How wonderful it is to have normal problems
Like a little delay in my pizza delivery
Or my grocery store being out of my favorite drink
Or my neighbor's dog excitedly barking at cars going by

How wonderful it is to have normal problems, as my full self,
human and hopeful
humble and proud
honored and alive
How wonderful it is.

BECAUSE AFTER ALL, HE'S JUST A MAN

MEGAN CANNELLA

you up, he texted. It was more command than question. This was her window. If missed, whatever blame he may be thinking of accepting would be irrevocably transferred to her.

Yeah, she responded immediately, because she just happened to be holding her phone when the text came through. He mistook this for forgiveness.

I need your wet pussy on my face, he replied. She mistook this for an apology.

You don't know how to have sex in a relationship, he condemned. You only know how to have one night stands. Silently, she thought again that she couldn't believe she had stopped basking in her slutty glory for this guy.

She held his cock in her mouth until they were both bored of him. He mistook this as her failure, and reminded her of it every time she looked like she might stand up and walk away.

You seem nice, he spat. He had quit drinking before he even met her, but she was sure the smell of stale beer overpowered his words.

Oh. If that's true, we probably have a bigger problem, she winced. She took a sip of her water. He mistook this for crying.

Hey you, he whispered. She was instantly suffocated by the expectation and by the history of his words.

When she describes this feeling to her doctor, she doesn't mention his name. Her doctor mistook the feeling for generalized anxiety disorder.

Hey you, he said. She opened her mouth to respond.

She shut it, wordlessly. He mistook this for her still loving him, despite.

Hey you, he screamed in her face, his hands doing what they could to meld with her shoulders, so they couldn't be free of each other.

I know, she replied softly. I know. He mistook the tears running down his face as hers.

THE SWAMP

AISHWARYA KHALE

One moment of distraction.
She drags her body out of the Swamp; resolute.

Did I see a ghost?
I saw someone.

It's late. The bus stop reeks of petroleum.

I did. A woman.
You've been drinking.
I'm telling you.
Where?
By the Swamp.
Over the dam?
I know you think there's no one but I'm telling you what I saw.

***

The cricket ball follows the old path. Out by the Swamp.
The wind uncurls.

I heard her again.
Go back. Is it the summer buzz?
May be.
No... cannot be.
I am losing my sanity.

I can feel her crawling out of the Swamp.
She slithers onto the grass. Her hair tattered. Naked
She looks at me.

I see her worn body.
Is she still there?
Silence.

Her bosom heaves like wildwood. She turns around. Her bare back
facing me. She bends down. Touches the muddy water.

Home, she whispers.

***

The lady by the Swamp, mother says.
(Raped. Declared dead. 1982)

***

The storm lingers on the horizon.
I sit by the tamarind tree.
I wait. For her.

Do you want me to sing you the
Blues?
She nods.
The melancholia of the tune pierce through her ears.
Crying, she looks at them in the reflection of the Swamp's
water.
The moon rise likes a moth.
Blood bleeds between her legs.

She spreads them and looks down at herself.
I turn around and look the other way. She heads towards
the water.
twenty-seven seconds…

She is sitting cross legged.
I stand still.
An hour passes by. She doesn't speak anything.
I walk towards her. Sit by the trunk.
Our shoulders touching.

She has scratches on her inner thighs and her breast.
Her nails bitten. Fingertips swollen.

I can't make myself look at her. I want to see her.
A gush of wind. She puts her hair behind her ears. She turns
her back to me again.

There are knots in her hair. I touch them.
She doesn't fidget.

I section them. I tie a loose braid.
I ask her if she wants flowers in her hair. She nods.
I bring her a yellow flower and put it in her braid.
We sit sound.
Our bodies becoming dust.

She looks up at me. Gets up.
Blood drips down her legs.

She gets down on her knees and hands, crawling through the mud,
once scarred limb at a time; and swiftly disappears
into the Swamp.

I'll come back again.
My words echo in the silence.

The yellow flower floats.
She disappears into the Swamp.

OLD WAY OPEN

KAYLA KING

This begins cracked and shucked
clean of feeling. And they will tell you not to write
about such things, about yourself as a thing

from memory. Yet, time
still moves. And you won't hold a child
to the Styx because there will be no children.

Eat away at chaos you can't control;
you are not the universe,
but you hold a bit of it inside.

They check for a new cosmos
amidst black holes hungry for filling.
Starched gown unlike feathers,

surround metallic beak to break
open. It's the way of an oyster,
sound a song only sirens sing

to seek something other than love.
They do not understand how
they survive: the nape, the vague,

the breast, the bone. You don't wear
flower crowns, but your hair is a nest.
And your mind is a wild shudder,

still starved. The strange lie
will find you in a painting
strung up in a room,

in a hospital, in a home.
Because there was beauty born
from brutal taking.

But do not trace the skin of the shell shattered
from a lost archetype, destroyed for its deceit
of that one word you refuse

to use. You'll become nothing
but a myth, a hiss to forget
forget forget.

THE WOMBING

AMANDA HURLEY

Cold wind blew through the market square. Margarete stood shivering, loosely clad in a dress a size too small that the overseer had pulled from a sack an hour before. There was a rip on one side and a rusty stain at the hem that could have been blood, but Margarete was too frozen to notice. The dress provided no protection from the wind, nor the icy grains of snow it carried within.

Margarete was third in the line of women who waited in silence for their turn to mount the roughly erected stage that dominated the market square. The noise of the gathered crowd sounded sharp to her ears. Despite the early hour, most of those gathered were enjoying the auctioneer's free whiskey. Drunk men were likely to pay more for their wares and glasses of cheap amber liquid were being passed around freely. Margarete was thankful for the broad back of the woman standing directly in front of her, shielding her from the catcalls of the men who were shoving and pushing each other for a glimpse of the women.

There was a sudden roar. Over the cheers, Margarete heard the sound of the auctioneer's voice, welcoming the men to the sale. It starts now, she thought, as the overseer hastened towards the front of the line, slipping the shackles from the feet of the first woman. Though the noise of the crowd had quieted during the introduction, now it increased in volume as the woman was led to the stage.

Margarete had seen her the night before in the cell where all the women had slept. She was small and pretty, no more than thirteen. The girl spent the night sitting by herself, rocking on her heels, a thumb firmly wedged in her mouth as if regressing to childhood actions could provide some kernel of comfort.

98

"She'll be taken quickly," the woman in front of her muttered, half-turning towards Margarete and mustering her figure. "As you'll be. God help you both."

Margarete searched the stage. The first young girl swayed next to a large man dressed in a suit, a black top hat placed jauntily on his head. The girl looked close to fainting, her lips blue with cold and knees half-bent, as if no longer able to carry the scant load of her slight figure.

The auctioneer turned and gestured toward the girl, pointing a curled finger at her fine long hair. Then with a sudden movement, the auctioneer ripped the thin dress the girl was wearing, exposing her chest to the gathered men. The crowd's silence was sudden, as if collectively, the men forgot how to breathe.

And then the bidding began, offers of money coming loud and fast for the girl, who clasped the ragged edges of the dress over her breasts.

The older woman had been correct; it didn't take long for the hammer to fall. Led away from the stage, the girl wept.

As the overseer hurried over to the line, the older woman turned again to Margarete.

"Time to give 'em something to really look at!" she cackled. Thrusting her face closer to Margarete's, she added softly, "If I were you, I'd take the first glass shard I could find and slit my wrists."

Shaking off the overseer's hand, the older woman clambered up onto the stage, walking confidently towards the auctioneer. Without missing a beat, she lifted her skirts and spun on one foot, pointing her naked derriere toward the crowd. Hoots of laughter and jokes greeted her as the auctioneer rushed to rearrange her clothing. Shrugging him off, the woman turned and unbuttoned her shirt, exposing a scarred, breast-less chest. The laughter turned to jeers and angry calls of "Cheat" and "Git her outta here!"

As the elder was led from the stage in a hurry, she turned to look back at Margarete, raising a gnarled finger and dragging it across her throat.

And then she was gone, disappeared from view.

When the overseer prodded her with a stick, Margarete realized the shackles on her ankles had already been removed. Hesitantly, she began to climb the steps to the stage, fighting a desire to clasp her hands over her ears as the shouts of the gathered men became even louder.

The auctioneer took a step toward her, a look of pure greed on his face, mentally calculating the profit Margarete could bring him. She stopped just out of his reach and turned to face the crowd. A selection of faces emerged: a man with a shaggy beard, broken teeth set in his jeering mouth, another with cheeks blistered from the cobalt mines, a faint blue tinge to his skin. And next to him, a harder face, richly handsome with cold, sober eyes. His gaze trapped her on stage, as if every other person present had suddenly vanished. Even after the auctioneer took her arm, Margarete still felt ensnared by the man's stare.

"A fine young specimen, gentlemen!" the auctioneer called, fumbling at Margarete's dress. "These pretty udders will certainly attract a pretty penny. Who'll start the bidding?"

Margarete stood exposed on the stage. A jumble of voices shouted, each with a better offer than the last.

Finally, a cold, clear voice rang out, trumping the bids. "Five and a half thousand for the maid."

Instinct identified that voice, and Margarete knew it belonged to the man who'd seized her in his line-of-sight minutes before. Gasps of surprise echoed around the market square. Margarete winced as the auctioneer's gavel hit his desk.

"Sold! Congratulations, Mr. Garvey. Only the best for you, sir!"

At the bottom of the steps, a coach pulled up with a jangle of reins. Margarete had only a moment to notice the two sleek horses before being pushed roughly inside. She collapsed on the floor, shivering despite the warmth of a soft fur beneath her exposed skin. She knew he was there with her before opening her eyes.

Even sitting, he towered over her.

Mr. Garvey.

* * *

Perhaps it had been the drug Mr. Garvey pressed into the crook of her elbow or the terror of the past few days, but Margarete woke from a sleep thick with dreams of green fields and animals. Among them were cows, sheep, even horses; animals only vaguely remembered from books had been clearly detailed. And now, there was a softness lingering on her fingers, as if she had been running them through a velvety coat of fur.

Startled, Margarete sat up. She searched the small room paneled with wood. A low ceiling stretched above her, but below, she lay on a bare plank. Electronic equipment attached to the wall in a jumbled heap.

Margarete focused on her pale cheeks reflected in the blank screen of a computer monitor. She traced the point on her arm where a drip had been adhered.

She'd expected this. There were no surprises about what was to come. Since beginning womanhood with her monthly bleeding, it had only been a matter of time before Margarete was sold and sent away from the hatchery where she'd been raised. It was the same for all the girl-children, natural for them to leave, one after the other. Margarete learned not to become too attached.

During the fifth World War, fertility failed with the advent of a new kind of chemical weapon. Ever since, all females—whether human or animal—had become prized objects.

Now that she'd been purchased, Margarete's worth only existed in what her body could generate. Her monthly bleeding meant she was able to produce eggs, from which hatchlings could be grown.

The math was simple: twelve eggs a year for the next twenty-five years, harvested as soon as her body produced them. They would be taken to laboratories for fertilization, then the embryos would be nurtured in artificial wombs as they developed into hatchlings.

Margarete's own existence began in such a place.

No longer a hatchling, Margarete accepted her duty as she must. She lay back on her makeshift bed, head aching from the after-effects of the drug administered by Mr. Garvey. Already her body felt different – her breasts larger and swollen. She ran a tentative hand over them, feeling the veins pulsating under her skin. Her milk was starting to arrive. Her training prepared her for this process too. High doses of oxytocin would be given to replicate a pregnancy, to stimulate milk flow. That milk would be used to not only feed the hatchlings, but as an ingredient in beauty creams, available only to the richest men. Like Mr. Garvey. For a moment, Margarete wondered how many other women were kept in the neighboring rooms.

Without warning, the door banged open. Two elder women entered; eyes filled with scorn as they stared at Margarete's still-exposed body. Their shifts fell flat to the ground over flattened chests, amputees like the woman at the auction.

One turned to her companion. "Another milkmaid. That's the fourth new one this moon."

Margarete understood her resentment.

Women's value hinged on their ability to produce eggs or milk.

Once women became too old to contribute, their breasts were cut from their bodies, the soft tissue finding its way into facial creams. If the women were lucky, they would be kept on as servants or to provide pleasure for their owners. The unfortunate ones, like the woman at the market, were cast aside.

There were very few women who earned the right to a natural death. Margarete shuddered, thinking about how the woman must have suffered after the auction.

The two women paid Margarete no mind, bustling around the room. The first, with long greying hair, checked the oxytocin levels in the drip, ensuring the proper placement of the cannula in Margarete's arm.

The second, shorter woman picked up an iron shackle from the ground and placed it around Margarete's elbow, securing it in place with a solid padlock. A hole in the middle accommodated the drip, while the other end of the chain bolted to a ring in the floor.

Once finished, the second woman pushed Margarete back onto the bed, fastening straps around her neck and stomach, effectively tying her to the bed. The tattered dress, which still draped around her waist, was removed while the grey-haired woman switched on the computer monitor and began running an ultrasound wand across Margarete's womb.

"Egg's a few days away," she told her colleague as a blurry image appeared on the screen. "Schedule a scraping for Tuesday."

With an officiousness borne of practice, the grey-haired woman then pulled at the equipment fastened to the wall above Margarete's head. Margarete gasped in shock and pain as two cups attached to long tubes were clipped firmly to her breasts.

102

As a button on the wall was pressed, the pumps began to vibrate. Margarete groaned as the cups pressed tightly against her skin. There was a long silence and then slowly, yellow-white liquid flowed into the tubes before being deposited into a sterile container.

"She's a milker, this one," the grey-haired woman said with a laugh.

"Garvey will be pleased," her colleague added, turning her back on Margarete.

The amputees clicked off the overhead light before leaving the room, the door thudding closed behind them.

Margarete shifted beneath the straps, bound, and forsaken without so much as the glow from the monitor. "Please... please turn on the light," she whispered, but the amputees' footsteps echoed down the hall.

For all her training, she hadn't been prepared for the darkness.

WE DON'T SETTLE HERE

TIFFINY ROSE ALLEN

Sometimes I contemplate this existence
What is this body
What is this femininity
What is the flesh
That I'm trapped in
That limits me?
I seem to only write when I'm feeling hazy
Not trying to be lazy
I'm trying not to scream
But all I want to do is scream

I'm reaching inward for my Goddess
For my chalice of rising up and not settling
Not hardening

I hope the gods won't forsake me
For finding my solace when my heart is aching
I want to lay myself down in graveyards and
Feel the earth swallow me
I'm so tired
I'm so tired

But deep down I know
That I've got to keep fighting
I've got to keep trying
I've got to keep on
I've got to keep on
I've got to
I've got to

I can't let the world take my goodness I'm
Trying so hard to hang on
I'm not forsaken
I am strong

I am good
I'm okay

I'll get through this
Just like any other day

Take my dramatic life and show me what paradise looks like.

3,2,1, I count backwards
My body is formed from pain
We as women know so much pain
So, what do we do with it?

We take it
We channel it
We make it the very artwork that we are
We burn our incense and sing our songs
And keep on going amidst our grief
Our physicality, our loyalty, our spirituality.

I cannot speak for you but I can hold your hand as you rise
We can walk each other along the paths of
Finding.

We don't settle here.

WHITE BUTTERFLY

TEIGAN JAYMES

There's something about a whisper. The fragile pitch of a voice understands anything louder might destroy the world. Or rather, life as it's known in the moment. It's why I kept the music low. Juice WRLD croaked out *this is the end of the road.* And I cried without knowing why.

More than a delayed shift in seasons caused a chill to prickle my skin. I turned the heat higher in my car to shed the shiver. But it didn't matter. I was bone cold.

Early morning promised more time to think. My parents got on a flight headed elsewhere. I made my way back to my own house, bundled in a sweatshirt with the words *I am unwell.* Though I was working on getting better, the prescription for antidepressants remained too new.

Progress.

My therapist liked to remind me of this word in our sessions. Two weeks until our next appointment; no use in unraveling until then.

* * *

The spare test had been waiting since the Saturday before. The first I took alone: negative. Now two days late, I submerged the stick in the cup.

One line appeared.

I walked away.

A faint second line bloomed in the time it took me to return.

Desperate for reassurance, I dug through the garbage, settling the first test beside this new one.

There was something. However slight, the proof existed.

With both hands gripped on the bathroom sink, I waited for the room to cease its spin. Maybe the world would never feel steady again.

This wasn't how it was supposed to feel. Someday always seemed further away.

* * *

Before crossing the threshold into the bedroom, I memorized the stillness in the space. I stayed just beyond the doorway, tracing the chip in the paint from the slam of the door some many months ago.

I cleared my throat. "We have a problem." My words weren't a whisper, needing Robin to understand.

Though he slept in the bed that was no longer ours, he sat up. He rubbed his eyes. When Gomez emerged from beneath the blankets, tail wagging, Robin smiled down at him. It took a moment for Robin to find me in the darkness.

His smile disappeared. "You're pregnant."

"Don't tell anyone." I thought of the saying about the tree falling in the woods. If no one beyond the house heard the news, would it really exist?

Robin shifted to the edge of the bed. "This is going to be fine. It'll be okay." Only after the consolation did he agree he wouldn't say anything.

* * *

Once the hour turned over to 9AM, I took my phone to the car. This was a call I needed to make beyond the walls of my office.

After two rings, the menu options began. I chose to speak with someone, unsure of next steps. A woman answered with a soft voice. "Dr. Jackson's office. How may I help you?"

Without delay, I admitted, "I think I might be pregnant."

"Congratulations!" The receptionist's voice filled with excitement.

She scheduled an appointment with my gynecologist for June 24th, offering more congratulatory exclamations before the end of the call.

I wrote the date on a McDonald's ice cream wrapper salvaged from the bottom of my cupholder.

Counting the days between then and now left me with twenty-eight.

Did that same stretch of time transform a caterpillar? At the age of five, I picked milkweed in the backyard to fill a glass jar for the unit on Monarch butterflies. But thinking back, I couldn't remember if other small creatures took just as long to find themselves whole.

Without searching for the answer, I returned to work. The rest of the day forced me to go on as if some major shift hadn't transformed the feeling of existing in my body. One line from "End of the Road" still played in my head: *it's far from over, losing composure.*

Robin texted. "I need a pair of New Balance sneakers. I need dad shoes." He tried to make light of the situation.

Maybe he didn't feel the heaviness inside the way I did.

I couldn't ask, sending a different text instead. "I'll stop at the store on my way home to get another test."

He told me he would go instead. Once in Target, he called. "We should probably get an idiot proof one this time. Don't you think?"

I agreed from the other end of the phone.

The shuffle of cardboard against metal filled the silence as he perused the shelves. He cleared his throat. "So, well, I told Dempsey."

The name of his new girlfriend broke whatever okayness I'd mustered throughout the day.

"We agreed we wouldn't tell anyone?" It came out as a question. No matter how hard I tried to take it back, to add power to the reminder that yes, we had confirmed that morning, I couldn't manage more than a whisper. I would break beneath the weight of the disappointment. And it was too soon.

He bought a digital Clear Blue test.

One tiny word appeared.

Pregnant.

I looked up at him, noticing splotches of pink petaled against his neck.

He rubbed at the hickeys. "It was just one last time. One last hoorah. Before—" He left the bathroom.

I followed, unable to respond.

"That's why I had to tell Dempsey." He promised it was over now.

Those words settled between us, but nothing was ours anymore.

Control slipped from my hands. My nails sliced into my palms, trying to grip tighter. But there was nothing left to hold; nothing to salvage.

It was difficult for me to sift bullshit from fact when it came to Robin. He had a way about him that caused me to question whether the liquid in a glass remained half full or empty. His indecision about us, about me, forced fault lines. It wouldn't be long before whatever this was fractured beyond repair.

Experience reminded me the shatter would come later. It always did.

* * *

Anything or everything.

The debate rattled inside like pills in the bottle, which I hadn't taken since the day before last.

My sister sat on the edge of the porch. Her cup of coffee spilled steam toward the sky.

I leaned against the railing. The sun peeked through the clouds, warming my arms through my sweater.

Already a day had passed, and if I didn't speak the words, they would choke me. "I have to tell you something."

"Okay." My sister turned back, studying my stillness.

"What's the worst thing you think I could say right now?"

She sighed. "You and Robin are back together?"

I couldn't fault her guess. Robin and I had been on and off more times than anyone cared to count, least of all me. And it would've been easy to agree. But I needed to say the hard thing.

I needed my sister.

"I took a pregnancy test." My voice shook. I breathed in through my mouth and out through my nose. Though I knew that was wrong, it didn't matter. Nothing felt right. "And it was positive."

Without hesitation, my sister stood. The distance between us disappeared when she wrapped me in her arms.

My exhalation thundered into her shoulder. I didn't know how much time slipped by before I pulled away, trying to speak through tears. "Can we just pretend like this didn't happen? For the rest of the day at least?"

She nodded.

But the tree had fallen. Now she was in the forest with me. We heard the sound in different ways.

It couldn't be so simple.

* * *

A few years back, I drove this same road. The sun set over the lake. My sister framed me in the foreground. She took the photo on an older iPhone, but I still liked it. Our laughter reverberated like ocean waves, ears still ringing from the concert. Days didn't feel so destructive.

This was a different year.

Now we didn't speak above the whisper of my car's heater. Sky darkened overhead, transforming the lake into lead. Perhaps a storm approached. I drove us toward a coffee shop.

The night before we did our best to pretend, allowing whole minutes to settle into the chatter of others dining out. I knew only that I wanted the soft scrape of salt on my fingertips after each french fry. Other unknowns and possibilities threatened to steal that distraction from me.

When we arrived, I spotted Carolina leaning against the brick facade. "Looks like she already grabbed coffee." I smiled. Not having to leave the warmth of the car already made the morning easier.

My sister opened the door, offering Carolina the front seat. "Ready to go?" She didn't specify our intended destination because we didn't have one in mind.

When asked how I wanted this conversation to go, I requested a long drive. The forward motion of the road reminded me there was no going back.

Carolina slipped one cup from the cardboard carrier, handing it back to my sister. She inspected the top of the next before offering it to me. After adding her own coffee to the cupholder, she buckled her seatbelt. "Ready."

I signaled to leave before pulling away from the coffee shop. Unsure how to begin, I sipped from the foam spilling onto the lid.

"How are you feeling?" Carolina's voice softened.

I took another swig from my caramel latte, savoring the salt I requested on top. "I'm tired." I sighed. "Also confused. And overwhelmed. Any moment of quiet makes my thoughts louder."

"Let's fix that." Carolina queued up a playlist on Spotify. Once she plugged in her phone, the soft strum of an acoustic guitar filled the space. "If it's easier, I can tell you about my experience."

I nodded, falling silent along with my sister who'd yet to speak since we started this drive.

This was a route I'd taken in the back and forth from college to home years before. The familiar landscape passing by brought comfort and predictability, both of which I needed.

Carolina explained the test, how she broke down afterward, the conversations with her boyfriend, Orson, and other friends, my sister included. "The decision was easy for me. I wasn't ready. Orson wasn't ready. I made the appointment. And even though I knew I couldn't have that baby, I imagined life as a mother someday."

"And now?" My question came from a place of guilt, solidifying like a hot stone in the pit of my stomach.

"I know we'll have a family someday." She brought the coffee to her lips, taking a long gulp before returning it to the cupholder. "But I want you to know what I didn't."

I said *okay* after each part of the timeline: the ultrasound, the waiting room at Planned Parenthood, the insurance coverage, or lack thereof. The moment before and after the first pill to induce a miscarriage. Remaining pills taken at home. The additional prescriptions and supplies. Waiting. And when all was said and done, the moving on.

Beyond the window, the world bloomed with new life. It would be summer soon, but I couldn't think past this conversation.

Carolina changed the song in the shuffle. "They explain how you'll pass the clot, but they don't tell you what it will look like, how a split-second miscalculation can leave an imprint in your mind." Carolina took a deep breath. "And you'll grieve. I'll tell you that now. Loss is still loss, whether it's unexpected or you make the choice."

"I'm trying to keep Robin out of my head, to stay focused on what I want. But I don't think I'm there yet." When I picked up my cup, it was lighter than I expected. My latte was almost gone. After I

111

took the last sip, I turned the heat up one degree, already missing the warmth.

"Obviously my experience is not yours, but I'm here to answer any questions you might have later." Carolina rested a hand on my elbow as reassurance.

I nodded.

My sister had questions.

She pieced together what she remembered from the year before when Carolina went through this. Though I couldn't see her face in the rearview mirror, I knew it would be focused, formulating a plan for everything that needed to be done while I was still deciding.

"So, does it make sense for her to schedule an appointment with Planned Parenthood now? Even if it's just to talk about her options?" My sister's fingers clicked on her phone screen. In all likelihood, bringing a list to life in her notes app.

Carolina nodded, the movement mussing the hair from her ponytail. "They won't make you do anything you don't want to do. But it might be nice to talk to someone there. And they fill up fast with appointments, so even a day in the not-so-distant future might ease your mind."

After that, Carolina changed the playlist to something brighter.

I cranked the volume and rolled down the windows and allowed the wind to tangle my hair. The touch was a comfort.

For the next forty-seven minutes, we didn't speak. Once we made it to Crestview Ave, Carolina paused the music, and unplugged her phone. "This will be hard either way. I'm still working through everything, and it's been more than a year."

I took a shaking breath, feeling the noise and the fear building inside.

Before Carolina disembarked, she leaned over, and wrapped me in her arms. "Whatever you choose, you can do this. Ask for help when you need it. But listen to yourself first."

* * *

Nobody had time to fall apart these days. It's what I told myself during each conversation, clinging to the precipice of stability from one moment to the next.

Over Italian food with Robin, we decided we weren't going to keep the baby. I wasn't ready. He wasn't ready.

"I'm sure they'll understand when I tell them." He set his fork down.

The smell of burned garlic overwhelmed the restaurant. I breathed through my mouth. "Dempsey knows." Those words tasted bitter when I spoke them. To distract myself, I organized the sugar packets from white to yellow to pink in the dish between us. "Who else?"

"Well, Dempsey was behind the bar when I told the other guys at work. And my mom knows. You didn't drink any sangria at her birthday dinner."

I laughed at the absurdity. The sound strangled in my throat, edging toward a sob.

But I wouldn't fall apart. "Just great. I haven't even told *my* mom yet. And now all these other people who I've never met know about this?"

"It's not a big deal. This will all be okay." He reached for my hand across the table.

I sighed. "I don't know why I keep trying to believe in you. It's not worth it." When I pushed away from the table, the shaker of parmesan tipped, spilling powder-fine cheese. For a moment, I wondered if I should throw it over my left shoulder. But no, that was salt, right?

If my sister were here, she'd explain the intricacy of that superstition. But she was at her house.

My hesitation caused Robin to look up at me, holding out his hand once more.

Though if there was such a thing as bad luck, I had enough already. Leaving the parmesan undisturbed wouldn't change that now.

I didn't say goodbye, fearing I might mean forever. I wasn't thinking clear enough for something so permanent.

* * *

Distortion happened all the time. I understood the complications from misreading a situation or conversation. And really, as humans, we're incredibly selfish, and tend to interpret the world the way we want.

But what I feared from telling my mother was the possibility of losing her. And if that were the case, she couldn't be a ghost. I wouldn't have a hairpin haunting where she could slip through the veil for a second to tell me everything would be okay.

No.

I would be without a mother only because I fucked up.

"Not possible." My sister rubbed a hand on my back. "At worst, she'll be disappointed. But when it comes down to it, I think she'll just be sad."

We talked about Gomez then. He'd gotten a sunburn on his nose at the park. As it peeled, more freckles emerged. "I'm thankful for his company." Scrolling through photos of him snoozing in the grass melted my heart.

I felt a rush of warmth toward this baby.

Without acknowledging the feeling or telling my sister about dinner with Robin the night before, I moved to the next photo.

She looked away from my phone. "Watching you go through this; it's breaking my heart. But I'm here, okay? I'm not going anywhere."

"Thank you."

For the next twenty minutes, I narrated the photos, each of them taken during hikes with Gomez. That was our time together.

"He really looks like his namesake here." My sister pointed to the black fur surrounding his upper lip, just as she remembered from the Addams patriarch.

But I only noticed moss sheared from the tree trunk by Gomez two minutes before I snapped that photo. Just like all the others, I took that trip into the woods as an escape from Robin back when we were together.

I didn't explain this to my sister.

"Mom just pulled up. You'll be okay?" She rubbed my back once more until I nodded.

I locked the car door behind us, sneakers crunching over the gravel in the parking lot. I followed last into the restaurant. The salt-sweet smell of barbeque clung to every inch of the dining room. Led by the hostess, we made our way around the booths to a table on the patio.

The sky cleared for the first time in days. I shed my denim jacket, favoring the warmth from the sun on my bare arms.

From the other end of the patio, live music played. I appreciated the roar from the bass, as it dulled my thoughts. The conversation drifted away from me.

Mom pointed to the margarita flavors, ordering hers frozen and flavored with strawberry. "Can I have a sugared rim?" When she asked, the server made a note.

"I'll have a mojito, please." My sister didn't look up from the menu.

I made a point of inspecting the different cocktails before requesting a water with extra lemons and a Diet Coke with one lime.

"You usually get a peach bellini?" My mom pointed toward the other flavors.

I shook my head, and the server departed our table to start on the other drinks.

"I'm trying to stay away from sugar before my birthday next month." I hated the lie, but I would take it back before the end of the night.

I was sure of it.

Though I still didn't know which decision I would make, I hadn't been drinking. Robin's mom was observant, I'd give her that. And I'd stopped taking my antidepressants altogether after reading about the birth defects such a prescription could cause.

So, when the moments of near crumbling surfaced, I couldn't tell if it was simply a surge of hormones or the lack of stabilization my body missed from the prescription.

Perhaps my therapist would scold me if I told her about skipping doses. But I hadn't shared about the pregnancy or the momentary togetherness with Robin. I feared the words she would use. Landslide or backslide or trauma or love bombing or gaslighting or cataclysmic, maybe? But not *progress*. That had already been lost. If she didn't know, I could hold tight to the illusion that I was getting better.

Drinks and appetizers arrived in a blur. The dipping sauce I usually enjoyed with the fried pickles tasted off. All too soon, entrees were set before each of us. I started with the french fries spilling over the edge of my plate onto the brown paper table covering. If I had a pen, maybe I could've written the news beneath my mom's plate.

It would've been easier if time stopped, but wishing couldn't prolong the meal, and I'd made myself a promise that it was now or never.

My sister ate slower than usual. Perhaps she wanted something to keep her busy. I wouldn't remember to ask later, but I knew her well enough to guess at the delay.

I cleared my throat. "Mom? I have to tell you something."

"Okay." She rubbed my arm, waiting for the admission.

Unwilling to let tears spill yet, I swallowed them. My throat felt sticky. I looked down. "Don't hate me."

"I could never hate you. No matter what." Mom remained patient.

Water. Sip. Swallow. Breath. "I'm pregnant. And I don't know what to do. I'm scared and I know you would rather this be anyone else in the world like a random stranger, or a one-night stand. Whatever. But it's Robin's." Water. Sip. Swallow. Breath.

"It'll be okay." Mom held her arms open, allowing me to press my face to her shoulder like I'd done with so many heartbreaks and bad days before. This moment existed somewhere between. Or maybe it was that I'd numbed myself to reality.

But with my mom still there, even after the news, it felt like everything might actually be okay.

Though I omitted many of the conversations I'd had with Robin aside from the first one on the first day, we did talk about knowing other women who'd chosen abortion. They remained nameless in conversation. But it left me to wonder how many crossed paths included a situation like mine.

We pushed our empty plates to the edge of the table, but we didn't leave. The world around us appeared translucent as dusk set in, almost like underdeveloped film.

I'd always enjoyed photography.

Not so much the instantaneous images processed through Instagram. I loved the dark room, the sharp scent of chemicals beckoning from the back of the classroom in high school. It reminded me that some things took more time.

Maybe that's what I wanted.

More time.

To decide.

116

To wait.

To plan for better circumstances.

But my life wasn't a photograph. And I didn't have the luxury of time. Not really.

When Mom cleared her throat, I returned to the present conversation.

"I never wanted you girls to think less of me." Mom looked from me to my sister and back. "When I was in my twenties, I had an abortion. I was with the "skeleton" in my closet. And I knew I didn't want to be tied to him for the rest of my life." Her eyes gleamed, tears like dewdrops in her eyelashes. She took a shaking breath.

Both my sister and I reached across the table to take her hands. We remained that way as Mom talked about how her sister drove her for the in-office procedure, which contrasted so much of what we heard from Carolina a few days before. It was a different time. But she'd been just as sure as Carolina.

They both carried loss.

I didn't think I was strong enough to shoulder that weight.

* * *

The urge to run didn't happen all at once. My heart raced first, an unpleasant flutter that lived in my throat like a hummingbird. Or was it a canary? If I opened my mouth, would I shriek that this was not the time?

"Do you want to see?" The woman's question was soft. She didn't pry.

No. No. No.

I knew if I saw my baby, I wouldn't be able to go through with this today.

"Yes." The word was near breathless.

She nodded and turned the monitor toward me.

I thought back to ink blot tests, trying to make sense of the black and white and grey spaces on the screen.

"Here." She pointed to a small round shape. Too small to feel real.

When I shifted, the paper crinkled beneath me. I sucked in a breath, the sterile taste of antiseptic settling on the back of my tongue.

The flutter raged again, ready to scream.

117

What came out was garbled, but the woman smiled, and rested a hand on my arm. "It's okay."

Outside Planned Parenthood, Robin leaned against the side of his car. He waved.

Tears formed before I made it to him, clinging to the envelope containing the ultrasound photo. I didn't know why I took it or why I couldn't go through with this today.

The back and forth with Robin leading up to this June 11th appointment eroded inside me. I was sure the ultrasound would spot a damaged cavern instead of a womb with a baby inside.

When I got to the car, I stopped before his open arms. "I couldn't do it."

He sighed. "That's okay. It's okay." He hugged me, whispering into my hair. "This is good. We can be good. I promise. And our parents can help. It will all be okay."

"Can we go?" I searched for the well-paved road. If we didn't leave, my legs would convince me to take off. And maybe the run would've done me some good. Allowing me to force this memory from my system. Let it haunt the woods instead.

Robin moved around to the driver's side door, idly tapping on his phone. He didn't speak as he started the car. He rolled both our windows down, perfuming the interior with fresh mown grass instead of the wax scent of melted crayon that had lingered inside ever since I'd known him.

Though he took a different route, I counted down the minutes toward home, wishing to fall into the cocoon of blankets and darkness in my room. I leaned my head back, allowing my eyes to close.

Robin nudged me. "Grilled chicken club?"

Only a few minutes had passed, but he was almost up next in the drive thru.

"Actually, I'll have the Chick-fil-A sandwich and waffle fries. And a Diet Dr. Pepper, please." I smiled my appreciation, waiting not so patiently for the warmth of the fries to meet my open hands.

The car remained quiet until we had our food.

Robin pulled into a parking spot, sifting through the bag to distinguish his order from mine.

I gulped my soda. It tasted wrong. It was enough to make me cry, but I focused on the fries instead, knowing they would be perfect.

Slipping the first from the box assured me they had an impeccable ratio of salt today.

"I have to make a quick call." Robin rolled up the top of the bag and left the car. There was a curb a few spots away, and he sank down onto the concrete, phone pressed to his ear.

Inside, the music cut from the speakers, replaced with a ring.

Robin looked down at his phone before returning it to his ear.

"So, she had a Juno moment and couldn't go through with it then?" The girl's voice echoed through the car.

Dempsey.

The name was there on the center screen, and I couldn't look away, fearing this was my own mind conjuring something from suspicion.

But when I found Robin approaching, jaw clenched, I knew it was real.

He slammed the car door, throwing his phone onto the dash. Pinching the bridge of his nose, he forced deep breaths. "Look, I'm sorry."

"Funny how Bluetooth works, right?" I laughed.

My lungs burned. Or maybe it was heartburn from the fries and soda or maybe I would throw up. My ears rang. A chill prickled over my skin, though there was no wind.

Maybe I would run.

"Dempsey's just struggling with all this. We had something going, her and I, and she's having trouble letting that go."

"So, when you say Dempsey, do you also mean yourself? I mean, fuck. You're the one who keeps saying we could be good and that we can do this, but you're lying to yourself. It's honestly a fucking joke at this point, and apparently I'm the only one laughing."

And I was. I couldn't stop laughing because I knew if it transformed into anything else, I would shatter without any way to pick up the pieces.

"Just take me home."

"Let's talk about this." He had his hands on my shoulders then, trying to get me to look back at him.

"There's a trail that heads back to my house. I'll just go for a run." I tucked the envelope into my sweatshirt pocket and unfastened my seatbelt.

119

Robin locked the car doors. "It will take you two hours, and that's if you keep a steady pace the whole way home, which you won't. So, I'll drive you." He started the car.

True to his word, he brought me back home.

He followed me inside, but I didn't have it in me to fight.

I sank beneath the sheets, making no comment when he untied his boots, and joined me, remaining on what used to be his side of the bed.

I'm not sure when I fell asleep, but I woke up tangled in the blankets, face pressed to his chest, arms wrapped around him.

Even in sleep, he kept his hands at his sides.

It was always me trying to keep him in my grasp.

"Why don't you love me?" I whispered into his chest, but he shifted away.

Now awake, I searched for my phone, needing to know the time. How long had he slept beside me like nothing had happened?

Phone in hand, I pulled the blanket over my head, rolling onto my side away from Robin. I clicked the home button, illuminating the photo of a cocktail on a bar.

This was Robin's phone.

It was 6:22 PM.

Now that I knew the time, I should've returned the phone to the depths of the bed.

Instead, I spent the next thirty minutes reading text messages between him and Dempsey every day since May.

He never ended anything with her.

He just added me back into the equation.

The last few messages twisted in my near-empty stomach.

Call me back when you can.

She should just know that one fuck up doesn't mean you're back together.

Because you're not back together, right?

He'd responded earlier that morning before the appointment: *I feel like I'm stuck in this situation. And what if it's not what I want?*

I couldn't keep rereading that one message, incongruous with everything he said after the appointment this afternoon.

I scrolled up to a conversation from yesterday.

You have my coffee, right?

120

Robin had responded: *Of course! Oat milk, two sugars, cinnamon on top, and a caramel drizzle. Just how you like it.*

The memorization of her order pushed me from the bed to the living room.

I left his phone on the nightstand, took Gomez, and nestled him against my chest before falling back to sleep.

* * *

There was so much to miss. But at the moment, I grieved for younger days when I could fully stretch without fear of a charley horse.

I did my best now, moving Gomez to the end of the couch.

The house was quiet. Robin had never been one to snore. But I crept through the living room, avoiding the spot near the window where the floor always creaked.

Empty.

The bed: unmade.

Robin: gone.

I searched the window. Only my car sat parked in the driveway.

With the world cloaked in darkness, I had no idea how long it had been since I'd moved to the couch.

Gomez stayed sleeping, but I would need to take him out soon.

I found my own phone on the floor in the bedroom.

Two texts.

I'm sorry.

Do you want anything from McDonald's later?

I typed back. *Yes. Fries. Thanks.*

I'm first out, but I might help Tarek start closing.

It was already after midnight.

Okay. I closed out of the messages then, focused on Gomez yipping by the side door.

"It's okay." I cooed the all too familiar word before securing his harness.

I grabbed a lighter on the way out the door, illuminating the patio with citronella candles. I breathed in the sweetness, taken back to summer bonfires, and camping with my family.

Once Gomez sniffed every corner of the yard, we settled into a chair. Crickets chirped and he snored, and I didn't mind being outside. At least it wasn't the same as being inside alone with the memory of the day looming over every inch of the space I used to share with Robin.

When another hour passed, I queued up *Moana* on my phone, keeping the volume low so as not to wake Gomez.

You can find happiness right where you are.

Damn, that line would be stuck in my head all night.

Not because it felt true.

It needled under my skin.

This wasn't happiness.

I paused the movie, opening a new browser to return to the Planned Parenthood site. I made another appointment, this time for June 21st.

Ten days.

With the confirmation in my email, I pressed play on the movie.

Robin arrived closer to 3AM.

The witching hour, my sister would say if she were here.

He set the McDonald's bag on the table. "Closing took longer than expected."

The smell of whiskey overtook the dwindling candles.

He'd been drinking.

When he leaned down to scratch Gomez behind the ears, I noticed fresh hickeys on his neck.

"You're kidding." I tried to laugh, but the sound was sharp. As I stood, I clutched Gomez close to my chest. I blew out the candles.

At the door, I held too tight to the handle.

To the place I know where I cannot go.

Where I long to be.

The lyrics from another *Moana* song mocked me.

Unable to grasp sense from this situation, I turned back. "You have to be fucking kidding if you think you're going to come back here after everything and pretend like closing the bar is the reason you're late."

"Really? You want to have this fight now?" He rubbed a hand through his hair. "So maybe it was you I was talking about today and not her. Maybe you're the one who can't let go."

"You deserve each other. Because the way I see it, as a woman, she's a piece of shit for not letting us figure this out. And you're just a waste of fucking time."

I didn't move.

He paced the porch.

I sighed. "Everyone said I could do better. And they were right. So go back to her. I don't care anymore."

He moved closer. "Oh, but you do. And it's pathetic. I mean if you say everyone was right, and maybe they are, that just makes you someone who spent two years and however many weeks now wasting your time. You're pathetic."

We both knew what to say to hurt each other most.

I sank to my knees, clutching at my chest to keep the sobs from waking the neighbors.

He laughed, and it hurt to hear.

But when I looked up, I found him crying, too.

He struggled to speak. "I can't do this. Okay? I can't be the dad I need to be."

"You should go." I pressed palms to my eyes.

Before closing the door behind me, I gave him what his guilt needed to subside.

"I won't make this decision based on you."

Untrue.

But I conjured conviction.

* * *

Upheaval was a nice word to think about. The first syllable lifted itself free from the other two. Sometimes it was painful to let it echo in my mind. Other times, the word reminded me of my father.

"I guess, what I'm trying to say is, do you want someone who will put your future child through all the bullshit we went through as kids?" My sister stopped before the tree line. "It's going to rain."

"Put up your hood." I allowed Gomez to sniff his way to the trail.

123

My sister stopped beside me, holding both palms up. "Not close enough yet."

"It's not like I forget. But I don't think I remember him like you do. It's all too vivid in your mind. For me, the memories aren't so clear."

Like looking through negatives.

Even still, I knew she was right. And though she didn't say it, it made sense that she would use the thing we hated to remind me why an abortion would be the sensical choice.

However, I'm not sure our mom ever really loved our father the way he expected. And when it came down to it, I loved Robin. Tethered by the illusion of what we could be, perhaps, I didn't mention this to my sister now. I didn't share how our last fight ended.

She'd reminded me time and again not to let Robin factor into my decision. But I think she knew I couldn't let go, or else, she wouldn't resurrect someone she considered dead. And I know this because once she talked about the eulogy she crafted for our father the day she decided he didn't matter.

I couldn't blame her, though I kept in touch with him. The man who raised us was our real dad. What did blood and lineage mean when you could choose your family?

Choice.

Too many choices and possibilities clouded my mind in much the same way the sky did overhead.

It would rain for sure. But would it storm?

I could've dealt with a drizzle.

Storms were too much.

This was why I brought Gomez out of the house and into the quiet and calm on days when Robin tore through our space like a tempest.

The residual energy of our fight brought aftershocks like an earthquake. In the days since, he told me how much he loved me, how much he liked Dempsey. It was always another excuse or lie or wish or manipulation.

Gomez raced forward, but the squirrel in his sight climbed the tree first.

I understood what it felt like to keep running toward something out of reach. And maybe not telling Robin about the next appointment was my way of holding out hope that he would choose us.

"Did you know butterflies only live for three weeks?" I tried to keep my voice steady.

My sister stopped. "All that work for something so fleeting? It's sad."

I looked up at the branches overhead, searching for a sign shaped in the leaves. But there was nothing. "It's been three weeks since I found out. And you're right. I don't want my baby to have a father like that. I can't do this."

When the rain fell, it lifted the damp smell of earth from below our feet.

"Do you want me to go with you?" My sister turned to face me.

Water dripped down my face, hood left unused between my shoulders. "I need to do this on my own."

"But if you change your mind, I'm here. For whatever you need. I'll always be here." She held my hand, walking beside me through the woods though the rain persisted.

This was more than a metaphorical place filled with felled trees.

I'd said the words. My sister heard them because she was right beside me. It was easier to speak it in theory than imagine what it would be like when it happened for real.

* * *

Blame could become an illness if I let it consume me.

I clung to the thought on the way back to the car, carrying a brown bag.

There was a list of other items I needed tucked in my sweatshirt pocket. It was too warm for the extra layer, but I couldn't bear to expose myself to the world.

"What's that?" Robin pointed to the lunch bag.

"It's the other four pills I need to take when we get home." I opened the car door, sliding into the passenger seat.

He'd spent the drive here crying, begging me not to go through with it. But his words from last night echoed in my head: *I don't want this because it means having to deal with you for the rest of my life.*

He opened my door, bending to meet my eye. "I don't understand."

"I'll explain on the way to Target." I buckled my seatbelt, facing forward.

Once he started the car, I rolled the windows down, keeping a firm grip on the paper bag. I cleared my throat. "They gave me the first pill in the office. It stops the pregnancy. The other pills empty the uterus. I'll take those once I get home."

The breakdown was simplistic.

I could've talked about lemons and clots and maxi pads and prescription-strength Advil and Tylenol, about cramping and expectations for tomorrow. Then I could describe the importance of the next pregnancy test, another check-up to confirm my womb had emptied the way it was supposed to with these pills. Maybe there would always be too much, but I focused only on the next thing: gathering supplies.

Robin smacked the steering wheel. "I didn't think you would do this. But you only took the one, right? So, it doesn't need to be over. You can just not take the others, right?" He talked too fast.

But I understood.

"No. It's done." I took a deep breath. "I told you last night that I could do this on my own if I wanted. It's clear you never wanted this. In the end, I didn't either." That voice didn't sound like my own, and I heard the words again as if from a distance, already a memory.

* * *

In theory, damage was a funny thing. There were times when the possibility of repair could be assured and others when further demolition was required, clearing away the old to make room for the new.

I existed between possibilities. If I focused on the pain of it all, it was immense, evidence pointing toward total decimation. Breathe in. Breathe out.

I'd slept on and off since inserting the other pills. If I asked the clock, it would tell me it was tomorrow, but it felt only like the longest day.

126

I gripped my hands against the synthetic tackiness of the yoga mat to distract from the severity of the cramps, much worse than I imagined.

"Goodbye Yellow Brick Road" continued to play on repeat. The words washed through me as I cried. It felt like a cleansing.

With a breath, I shifted into an extended child's pose. Keeping my focus on staying still allowed me to get through the next line: *Maybe you'll get a replacement. There's plenty like me to be found.*

I didn't want Robin to know that I would never be able to listen to this song again. I thought of the takeout boxes now emptied and stacked on the kitchen counter. Maybe I couldn't eat Chinese food after this day.

"I have to go." He moved from the chair toward the front door.

I stood, extending my limbs in a languid exhalation. "You said you would stay."

The witching hour approached again. Inside, it felt like rain. It was difficult to evade the building tension in the space.

"Well, you said a lot of things. But here we are." His voice echoed in the small room, waking Gomez.

I wanted him to *want* to be there, to help me through this, I wouldn't beg, but I could crumble.

The shattering came.

I fell to the floor, unable to control the sobs. Perhaps the pills would expel everything from inside, leaving me hollow.

Robin stood beside the mat, towering over me. "I don't know why the fuck you're crying. You made this decision, and you have to live with this decision. I don't want to be here."

I gasped for air, unable to catch a breath through the expulsion of everything I'd kept hidden.

He went to the kitchen.

My breathing steadied. I wiped my nose on the sleeve of my sweatshirt, standing to meet in the light of the refrigerator.

Robin grabbed unopened White Claws from the bottom shelf.

"You've taken everything else, might as well take those." I gestured toward the front door.

I followed him out to the road, standing still in his headlights. If asked to explain, I would call this momentary paralysis. In my mind,

I told myself to move, but my limbs wouldn't take me away from witnessing the final break between us. It promised total annihilation and I needed to bear witness.

He got out of the car but didn't move closer. "Do I need to call someone for you?"

"You're free to go." It was the finality of his offering that allowed me to move one step and then the next and another until I could close myself behind the door.

I sank to the floor. Gomez greeted me with a kiss on the chin. I texted my sister and called my mom.

No answer.

No response.

I was alone.

There was no point to keep on this way.

Perhaps the time had come for further demolition.

Let someone else clear my personhood away, make room for something new.

Scrolling through my phone, I passed name after name. People had come and gone, and I never deleted them from contacts, and they wouldn't answer.

I called Ned. He was a nice boy from college who I hadn't spoken with in too many years.

"Hey. What's up?" He answered, voice filled with sleep.

The truth of the last few weeks and even the months before spilled out like a tsunami. It was almost 4AM. I was a stranger who wanted to end it all. I waited for the information to drown him on the other end of the phone.

He cut me off. "Look at Gomez. He still needs you. So, you can't go anywhere, okay?"

I nodded. Coughed. Cleared my throat. "Okay."

"Let's watch Schitt's Creek. You have Netflix, right?" The smile was clear in his words, though I couldn't see him on the other end of the phone.

I started from a random episode. I layered two blankets over myself, letting Gomez curl up under the first.

I blocked Robin's number.

Tethered to this other person, I felt my edges solidifying, my permanence in the world secured.

Ned stayed on the phone with me until I fell asleep.

* * *

Suppose it would've been poetic if three weeks had passed, but it'd been only two.

My mom and sister stood in the driveway at my house, both struggling to ask if I was okay because maybe they knew I wasn't.

But I believed I would be.

Someday.

It was a stretch of time I forgot about through the course of June.

Now it was July.

A white butterfly flew under the eaves of the porch, landing on my hand.

We didn't breathe, the three of us gathered in a semi-circle, waiting for the creature to fly free.

It felt like this was a message from my baby or maybe just the universe, letting me know it was okay. The guilt still gnawed sometimes, reminding me I could've done it.

Been a mother.

This butterfly didn't move.

I imagined the whisper of another butterfly's wings, unleashing the chain of events that would be bound only to memory now. Though delicate, did she know what she destroyed? And where was she now, that butterfly?

They only lived three weeks.

Beauty would always be fragile; I reminded my white butterfly.

But we both would go on.

SAFETY-SEEKING RITUALS

LAURA DOBSON

It was food / before it was fire
best befores examined / before
you'd take a bite / you've   never
had food poisoning / never never   will
this morning / you reach the   end
of the path / reverse
direction / descent was easy but it consumes energy
to climb / four flights of steps

you're back / telling him
it's the being in control that matters / he's telling you that's funny
                    I prefer to be / controlled
you're new flames necking / spirits
when he / reveals
what he means / what he wants
and you do it / he insists
it's *smoking hot* / he cries out
in pain   pleasure / screams
inside   outside your head / you're shown
videos he's captured / videos
he will *never share* but he might
strike
the match
at any moment / everything
feels tissue paper fragile / combustible
and oh   what shame / your mum

sits broken in the kitchen / swallowing
Propranolol / prescribed when the man after the man after
your dad / left
came back left came back left / you explain
you've forgotten something / *again*
she sighs because *why* / *aren't you more*
like your sister / her first

from Oxford / top
of her class / at the top
of the stairs / sockets
empty / her termination kept secret between
not-mothers / your tries-to-be perfect sister
bled bled and bled / cried cried and cried
you there to console her / *there there*
on the floor / of your bedroom
the plug / lies
prongs up / nothing
appears connected
nothing

apart / from **everything**

SHE FELL IN LOVE WITH THE RIVER, AND THE RIVER LOVED HER BACK

LINDSAY STENICO

after Ophelia by John Everett Millais

Such a strange girl, that darling Ophelia,
one who always loved too much,
or much too wrong,
who lingered out in gardens
for longer than was proper for a girl, at marrying age.

Suitors traveled the lands to seek her hand,
with love tokens held in honest palms
as they walked along the gravel path of
her precious garden,
only for her eyes to linger, seeking out the comfort
of the silken currents of the riverbed.

Such a strange girl who ran to the riverbed,
disclosing her worries to a bed of grass
under the protection of the tall willow tree
only for the water to sing her a song
while she *dipped* her fingers into its embrace,
then an arm,
going all the way up to her elbow
when the water turned warm, coaxing her
to stay as the late afternoon sun
burned in the sky
the longer she lingered in their secret place.

She declined the aster and Camellias,
despised the white and pink carnations,
and turned down even the rare chrysanthemum from
an all
too hopeful,
too loving,

too *human*, young man.

Instead, she made a bouquet out of ill desire.
Filled with butterfly weeds and purple hyacinth,
rounding it off with the last of the begonia
that sent the remaining suitors to foreign lands,
and drew the worried gaze of a mother out of women
without a child to their claim.

It was on the longest summer day
when the birds refused to end their piercing songs,
the flowers danced in an unseen,
unnoticed
breeze,
and she donned her finest dress to disappear
into the garden once more.

No one thought better until the strange bouquet
came floating its way
      down
        the
          river,

             and upon
     following the path, there in the water's warm embrace,
          was the darling Ophelia
       with twigs curled 'round her ring finger,
      intended for only the most sacred of vows.

THE LAST NYMPH

MARIANA FEYT

toe-tip forward
dipping in water
then springing out
the grace of a lout
threads through her moves;
she finds in grooves
the sum of her friends:
she laughs, pretends
that she's not alone;
under the dome
of the lower leaves,
her shoulders heave
with the force of sobs

STEREOTYPE

ADRIENNE STEVENSON

I try to please these desperate girls
that call on me from their dark corners

I give them silk dresses
turn mice to footmen, pumpkins to coaches
but what do I get in return?
no thanks or caresses for a tired old woman
who has spent her magic on the ungrateful wretches
no, they run off with the first prince
to pick up their dropped handkerchief or lost slipper

I will waste no more time on these girls
but return in my next incarnation
as a wicked witch
and enjoy myself for a change

WHITE SPELL

NICOLE TALLMAN

I'm that cat in *Constantine,*
but I'm also human and I'm talking,
casting a love spell with broken violins.

Crystal, smoke, stone—
I'm a mystic, a sage, a good witch,
a lucky 13 wearing a white gown.

Isn't a wish a spell?
I say: Lift the world's sadness.
I chant: Oṃ maṇi padme hūṃ.

Isn't a prayer a kind of magic?
Isn't silence?
Isn't the moon?

THIS IS HOW TO AFFIRM
YOURSELF

SLOANE ANGELOU

wake up everyday
pray to yourself
chant if you may—for you are many
say this:;

o woman i worship you
o woman o woman i praise you
o woman o woman o woman i adore you
you are precious
you are stunning
you are beautiful
you are magic

affirm yourself out of your misery
pour a love offering on your head
be tender to your heart
wear a smile on your face
do whatever it takes
wake up everyday
chant if you may—for you are mighty.

PYRO

KIRI DELANDÉ

I set fire to the wheat fields. Forgive me, they were so fertile—
so unabashed in their life-giving languor. Their golden stalks,
winking 'neath your vesper prayers, were practically begging to burn.

I drink in that nectarine skyline, licking soot from sour lips. I taste
metal, I taste rust. I taste a memory that could've been. They tell me,
this could've been something beautiful. It could've saved lives.
It could've brought comfort. It could've cured cancer.
But it would've ruined me.

I bloody my palms with crushed chrysanthemums, crack my knuckles,
croon with that calm kindling. You must look at me and see a monster.
Coal-cruel eyes, sin-sharp teeth. A mirthful smile that delights
in this death.

I mothered these crops, didn't I? I supplied the soil, lifted them with
my lifeblood; my body cowed to their cultivation. But maybe women
are just that wonderful; we create without even wishing it.

This is my miracle to mutilate. My day in the broiling,
hellfire sun. As you burn, I burn too, little ones. When
they gave me the match, they spoke of the pain. *There
will be blood,* they say, chewing chastity, spitting saints.

As if that would stop me. I swallow hemlock, pollute
my sweet earth. I have blood in spades to spare.

WITCHES

J GEORGE

I brew my tea like witches with their cauldron
with the essence of dried spearmint,
tender tulsi, powdered turmeric, crushed pepper and minced ginger
as the clouds read my day.
Little glass jars that vesseled ground coffee earlier,
now homes these healing herbs decorating my water altar.
For breakfast, again I turn to liquid food,
smoothies and shakes in plentiful color,
green, red, maroon,
for calm, serene, quiet in my dictionary.
During the cusp of each day,
when the bubble of the red cherry sun dives in and
resurrects as a silver ring of moon
I arch my back to touch my feet
and roll it to a ball, holding myself to be a pearl.
I brew my life like the witches,
wild herbs and weeds, dances at night and dawn
chants of affirmation and perspiration,
like the witches,
only I don't own a cape or a hat or the gown,
but I own my body and the magic to heal it,
like the witches of history.

THICK AS HONEY

THAINA JOYCE

I adore you because you are mine—
thighs, thick as honey, juicy as a cherry
tree. You're the house of history, the design
of my heritage. Your truth etched in stretch
marks, poetry in your cellulite. Society taught
me to despise you for swallowing
my shorts, taking my dress for a ride
up the hills of my hips. Thick girls never
made the magazine covers. I've clenched
shame between my knees, afraid you were taking
up too much space. I grew
to love the gaps you've filled, the trends
you've ripped. I've undressed you
for the summer—skirts above the knees,
I call it liberation. You allowed
the rest of me to take up the space it needs,
and the world will adjust.

IZIBONGO FOR BLACK WOMEN

KAI COGGIN

a praise poem, after JP Howard, for my Sisters

praise you Black Woman
because you never be praised enough
let me lift your collective name here
let me strip you of all your forced-on shame here
praise you for the stars that unfold when you smile
praise you for the way moons rise in your eyes
praise you for your tragic hope and sacrifice
life for you ain t been no crystal stair
but you still keep climbin on
praise Langston's mama
praise her wisdom and truth

praise you Black Woman
because you never be praised enough
praise be your laugh
let me say that again because it's the song
that makes the planet spin
praise be your laugh
how it cackles and coos loud brassy beautiful
unafraid and unbroken
honey and fire

praise you Black Woman
because you never be praised enough
praise your natural hair and its curls
how whole galaxies swirl in the furls of you
praise your box braids and your twist outs
praise your locs and your bantu knots
praise how I got a Sister whose afro blocks out the sun
praise how I got another Sister whose afro is so tall
God uses it for a microphone

141

infuses her as gospel
Black Woman
praise your fingers braiding and trading beads
and weaving histories into wild glorious hair
the ceremony of pulling
praise your pulling
praise your pushing
pushing back on all that no longer makes room
for your crown
here Queen—here is your crown

praise the Motherland of your womb
how everything comes from you
and is stolen from you
and is returned to you again in glory
or entombed
praise Breonna Taylor right here
I can't begin to know your story but
praise you Black Mama
forgive us for what we have done
and all that we still do
how we don't do right by your Black sons
how they are followed all their lives
by the shadows of guns
and how your Black daughters atlas the weight
of systemic cycles yet undone
and you still teach them to lift their faces to the sun
praise Breonna Taylor right here

praise you Black Woman
how you still raise continents of sons and daughters
despite their predisposition to being slaughtered
how the Atlantic Ocean is still found in your transatlantic tears
the salt of you betrayed and splayed out
creating lands under your feet from all your centuries of grief
praise you as homeland
praise you as shore of a brighter world
praise the holy map of you
praise the North Star
that hangs from your earlobe like a pearl
praise you Black Mama
for how you hold the world
praise your swaddle and thick body

your warmth and your song
how you lullaby the night with a defiant hope.

praise your hope
praise your dreams
praise the scripture of your face
praise the lines on your hands and crows-feet hymns
make an altar of my tongue
so that my words are poetic reparation
burn nag champa and sage in praise of your fire
praise be your fire
praise your persistence and your resistance
praise how you Harriet your children to a new freedom
praise how you Rosa until someone else offers you a seat at the table
praise how you Audre deliberate and afraid of nothing
praise how you Maya rising and phenomenal
praise how I got a Sister who named her daughter Revolution
Black Woman praise you
how your heroes and saints speak to you from the edge of the world
how your ancestors tell you the mountaintop is near
how every step toward freedom
is emblazoned into your DNA
encoded in your retaliations of Black Joy
praise your Black Joy
praise your Black Joy

praise you Black Woman
because you never be praised enough
praise your hips
praise your thighs
praise your arms and your legs
praise your back and your heavy head
praise your neck and them tight-ass shoulders
praise your temples
and how your whole beautiful Black Woman body
is a Temple
praise you Black Temple
praise your knees and your elbows
your fingers and your toes
praise your perfect beautiful Black nose
and your perfect lips
praise your voice that sings and hums and *hallelujahs*
praise your voice that shouts for justice

that leads us all to shout beside you ***BLACK LIVES MATTER***

Sister praise you
praise your heart for all that you bear
praise your ears for all that you hear
praise your eyes for all that you see
how your eyes and ears sometimes
bring you your biggest fears
and yet somehow somehow you soldier on
praise you Black Woman
I don't know how you be so strong
I don't know how you be so strong

this praise poem could just go on and on and on and on
because Sister—you never be praised enough

WE'RE ALL UNDER THE SAME SKY, BUT EVERY VIEW IS DIFFERENT

ASHLEY MARIE EGAN

A voice calls to me from the woods
she sounds familiar but obscure,
like a polaroid that was shaken too hard
how the memory distorts with the photo,
her voice rings in my head like a broken siren
at night her whispers are a dissociative lullaby,
I disconnect from my body to roam with her
a wisp of a woman and a disembodied voice,
in that form, there is no fear weighing me down
and my Plath oven-headed days feel mummified,
my feet tingle with memories of treks traveled
without Pandora's box flooding my mind,
I've got maps etched into my bones
but lately, I've been trapped in my home,
mind's been lost in the clouds
heart's been sinking like a stone,
but in the dark, I'm a nameless beast
a wild thing with adventure in my teeth,
I discover my fire still burns there
on a pyre of all my desire's to live,
I am the oxygen seeping from the trees
my heart won't grow cold as long as I breathe,
she encourages me to reclaim my youth
to damn the numbers and years buried,
all those ages I wrestled with my truth
slept on the edge of a knife with a pillow noose,
how the ink in my pen turned to blood
and every poem depicted an internal war,
how a finger gun used to click in my skull
to silence monsters still under my bed,
now my days are spent clinging to life
even if it means the absence of one,
I long to do more than grow old and gray

but lately, I've been trapped in my brain,
she is the adventure in my blood
that I pretend I don't have but I do,
can't tell if she's the past or the future
or something in between,
but when she talks every
sky I'm under feels like home,
with her, I don't feel hopeless
but only my mind wanders out the door,
and hope is a dangerous gamble
a wish made with no premise,
but I have it all the same
so I will share her road,
or maybe find one of my own
for life is futile without change,
and whether we want to or not,
we change all the same.

THE OTHER WOMAN

ELIZABETH M. CASTILLO

The sun has set, and at this hour,
shadows hang between the daylight and the trees.
There, the sudden scent of blood,

                    scent of *man,*

carries to me on the breeze, the wind
howling through, falls silent at my feet:

                good hunting, milady,"

it whispers, then retreats. There is
a darkness in this forest, an end
that rivals death itself,
in the mist about my ankles. Even lizards
know they would do well to hide
inside their hovels, and underground.

Dirt crunches beneath.

                Treacherous soil!

Leaves plunge downwards,
to be eaten by the earth.
The naked trees testify: this forest is deadly,
and will swallow you whole. I hear
footsteps racing, running, in thundering lockstep.
Flash of black. Flash of teeth.

                There are dangerous games afoot!

Surely it's time to turn back. Surely it's time to go home.
I am well beyond my borders now.

She can't catch me, she can't catch me,
here, where I lurk
and linger on the periphery
just out of sight, just beyond her mind's eye.
She knows I am here, her veins
course with rage, and vengeance.
But she does not know where.

                She is death. She is danger.

But the line has been crossed,
the threat prowls within
her marked territory.
She may think I have lost,
but this no longer bears any resemblance to a fair
fight. No, now two legs, not enough.
I drop down onto four,
draw strength from the thousand invisible
heartbeats, the lifeblood,
the microbiome of the forest floor.

There is fear, and some fury,
encrusted under each hungry claw. The hunt
smells of my father, champion long before I
had ever heard of this sport, and I wonder:
                              would he be proud?
There is sweat at my temples, and my wrists are bound
to stop them from trembling.
I step, crabways, low and feral, without shadow
or sound. Your ears twitch and you shudder,
neck craning to see what you
and I must learn the hard way:

                    the deadliest thing in here is me.

THE STRENGTH OF A WOMAN

ASHLEY MARIE EGAN

A woman's strength / is always described / as this delicate trait: / the courage of her / empathic heart / or the bravery in her / vulnerability. / These statements are true / but they're not the whole story. / Not all of our power / is as fragile as a flower. / What about the resilience / of every bloodied woman / who stands back up / after being beaten down? / What about the grit / of every ravaged woman / who faces her rapist / in the court of law? / What about the fortitude / of every degraded woman / who suffers in silence / and heals on her own? / What about the brute strength / of every expecting woman / who opens her body up / for another soul to enter the world? / Think of all the women / who got us to where we are now. / Think about how they / armored their soft hearts / for battle. / Think of how they stood / how they spoke / how they fought / because those women fought / for everything we have / and we will keep fighting / for equality / for freedom / for safety / for the next generation of women / to have more than we have now. / So that one day they may walk down the street / whether it be night or day / and never once / feel like prey.

THIRD PERSON

I am what they call a gold-digger. I don't mind—there is nothing wrong with choosing this path for oneself, just like there is nothing wrong with my husband's self-declared indifference to this fact: ours is a green card marriage, you know? I've never been in love in my life; I have an inclination toward equilibrium in all matters. But I love my husband in my own way, and I'm not deceiving him at all. The man is seventy and he does not speak to any of his immediate family. *A bunch of gold-diggers*, he says. At least you are courageous enough to say it to my face, he tells me. There's a real sense of companionship found between those who can be unapologetically honest with one another.

We are all diligent hypocrites, and that's our fate; to be hypocrites or at least one of the confused people who keep changing their mind. I change my mind too fast to register that in thought, though. I'm nothing but a cluttering of words and that makes me dizzy. I must form and perform as a persona so that I do not disappear in myself.

It is both a curse and a privilege—or rather, a fortunate catastrophe for the human species—those words shall never stand still; they will swim and drown and die on you. My words here are being knocked down like excited dominos waiting for their turn, with the violent grace of soon-to-be extinguished continuity of impression. If you talk too much, that's probably a good thing—but it is God's punishment to the wise that their words should still be repeated even after losing all meaning.

Is it that white sort of nothing? No, because that would mean nothingness can fill one's life up. But nothingness doesn't spill or leak or fall—nothingness escapes. Yes, that's the world. We've all felt it escape, and felt it missing, whatever nothing is, and that is why it's

150

nothing at all. It's simply a loss of words, and without words, nothing is what we get.

What I feel, nevertheless, is quite a lot, enough to fill a whole house, and it's another kind of white. It's a sober environment, maid-supervised kind. It smells like a hotel. It's self-satisfied boredom.

Every now and then I can go to the pool and read a book, or flirt with the idea of getting a second Wi-Fi. And I write inside that world, thinking it real and friendly; I wrote about this whole other inexistant world. And the maid is always cleaning something, and I have to keep moving from room to room as she cleans. I don't like her in there, not because I don't like her, but because she ruptures my sense of privacy. She invades my space and probably sees it in an entirely different way than I could ever bare to see it, and that space belongs to me, not her, and I will see it how I like.

But let's not pin it all on the place—the thing is, I just ran out of personality. Yes, I used to be funny once upon a time, but I can't even remember those times by my own eyes-in the memory film, I see myself in third person, talking and laughing. Certainly, this cannot be healthy, for one to see oneself in third person. Clara, I see her, at the age of twenty-two, hanging out by the pool.

Why do I keep thinking of myself in third person? There is I, right now, and there is you, which is whom the I in the mind addresses, and there is her, who is a thing of the past; or rather a thing of the future. She just isn't here, and it is impossible to summon her. And yet she controls my life. Every action of mine, every thought and decision; I wonder what it should mean for her, my third person; what that would make of her. She is much greater than me, and better, and worse, and smarter, and coarser, and angrier and nicer, too. She is very blurry to me, as she probably is to most people. And she exists for many people. I only exist for myself. For her to be real, I would have to disappear completely. Dissolve into a part. Stop having so many questions and forget about myself as a thinking organism. What a dream that is.

I realize that who I am in the future is a different person. She will be so happy and calm, and she'll be looking back at me, smiling at my naivety. I am not her; she has probably murdered me and dressed up in my skin just like the wolf did with the lamb's wool, and like the woman in some soap opera my mother used to watch. I was always very scared of her; the woman in the soap opera who killed a man's wife and dressed up in her skin so she could finally have him, the man. Soap operas are very philosophical in their own, far-fetched, way.

I am aware that to other people, I'm *that woman,* the very disagreeable one who doesn't come to parties. High society ladies do not like me for being a gold-digger. My husband's kids don't like me for that, and also because I'll inherit their money. I imagine that song, "The Lady is a Tramp," is about me. I always wondered why Ella Fitzgerald sang the chorus that way if she was signing in first person, but I know now. Ella, by the way, means "she" in Portuguese. So I guess she kind of was a third person, too. And she didn't care about what Frank Sinatra sang about her in his slut-shaming version of that song. See, Frank sang "I never bother with people I hate / that's why the lady is a tramp." There is also that part where Ella says, "won't dish the dirt with the rest of the girls / that's why the lady is a tramp." When Ella sings it, it's almost like a social critique. How little it takes, for a lady to be a tramp, right? And you know what, Frank? I like being a tramp. My hoe bohemia really is the place to be even if I am all alone when I lower my lap—that's how I prefer it, in fact.

I am a solitary person; I don't mind being alone much. I grew up with three very loud brothers and shared a room with my mother and grandmother and then only with my grandmother when my mother died. I had little to no privacy and whenever I got some money, I spent it on a hotel room. No sound to me is more pleasant than that of a door being locked. People always told me my family led a perverted lifestyle, as if we were in Zola novels and had been corrupted by poverty. But there's a lot of dignity in poverty, you see; there is dignity in hard work. Too bad it sucks.

Look, I enjoy a comfortable life. Had I not married Stevie, I'd be buried in student debt right now. An Ivy League education is never cheap, no matter how cheap their students. Yes, I am quite respectable in that league educated way. I have worked hard all my life, and I deserve this break. Only I majored in Ancient Greek, an impractical career choice—so you can see why I had to marry rich.

The thing is, there are people who are born rich, and then there are people who are born to *be* rich. Richness is wasted on the first instance; they give it no value whatsoever. They will spend their inheritance on dispensable stuff such as helicopters and yachts, not to mention parties and decorating and things made of gold and silver. God, they are helplessly idiotic.

Stevie thinks I'll do good with his money once he's gone. He says I won't spend it on superfluous things. This marriage may be imperfect for some, mine, and Stevie's but at the heart of it lies a true lime-mindedness.

Apart from my going on the occasional shopping spree, I am a bargain of a trophy wife. I do like spending money on frivolous things, do not get me wrong, but when you got lots of money, the satisfaction isn't quite as great as the one experienced than the less fortunate. See, shopping to me used to be quite a self-destructive activity I indulged in, but now that I find myself in no financial trouble, it has lost its dangerous glow.

Still, I need some sort of addiction. I need some sort of conflict in the middle of my calm, comfortable, exhausting life. Not the Madame Bovary sort of conflict, but some sort of complexity of spirit which would render my life vivacious. Which is redundant, considering vivacious is just another word for lively, and to say one wishes for a lively life is moot.

Stevie enjoys fishing.

He's not the stereotypical rich man. He hates golfing. He says he's a simple soul. When I went with him one summer, he picked up a fishing line, and threw it with hook and bait under the water, beneath the boat. He built his boat himself; he has no time for boat shopping. If he's ever stranded on a desert island, he'll know how to get out. Stevie is obsessed with exit plans. He always gets seats next to the emergency exits and he has a stun gun in case there is a shooting out of nowhere. It happens sometimes in places we aren't, in the alternate reality of the news, with all its unidentified shooters who were bullied when they were kids.

So, Stevie enjoys fishing.

Last time he took me on a trip, we just heard the ocean speak in its ancient mermaid sounds, which was probably the sound our souls made way before we were made into this people mess—it must've been nice, to be a solitary soul swimming in a river. Or maybe it's best to live in a boat made of wood in the unknown.

I wonder who is responsible for guarding words, to make sure they don't disappear. I suppose it would require a great deal of triage—take a disappearing word, such as, say, *cerulean*, which is the color of deep sky blue, and compare to another one, such as *divagate*, which is the same as digress, and pick one to save: cerulean versus divagate. The latter is clearly the right choice, if not for its meaning, for its resonance.

Saying deep sky blue is way more beautiful than saying cerulean; cerulean is an affected, overly scientific word disassociated with its attempted meaning. See, the trouble with some words is, they are too ambitious. They try to hold an entire world of definitions inside them, and they turn out empty. No, the best words are basic words like *though, do, have,* which despite their many uses, never confuse you when properly applied.

It is, however, sentences that hold meaning, not words; not words at all. Otherwise, we'd be making a tangle of half symbolisms wherever we went—when I tell you my husband raises the fishing pole in order to gain impulse and throw it into the water that is not to be interpreted as symbolism for a dick. It's about a fishing pole—still, I'm pretty sure a hundred Freudian scholars simply saw the words "raise" and "pole" put together and decided this was about a dick.

And, you know, what is it about literature and dicks? It was all very well and modern in the 20s, but by now, we should have lost this obsession with phallic symbols. Why can't a dick symbolize a fishing pole or an elevator lever or anything that has been used to subtly suggest phallic forms, instead of the opposite? Also, since we are on this subject already, I would like to formally petition the guard of words, whomever he or she may be, that the word "erect" and all its variables be removed from our verbal history. No words is more redundantly suggestive than that.

Anyway, that being said, I do believe that my husband's favorite book, *The Old Man and the Sea*, is about dicks. When I shared my opinion with him, he laughed in my face, and I told him the whole thing was an allegory for Hemingway's difficulty to deliver a satisfying performance in bed. Since *The Sun Also Rises* is about impotence as well, though in a much more direct way, it is safe to conclude that Hemingway had issues regarding his penis, which is also why he so cruelly exposed in Fitzgerald in *A Moveable Feast*.

"When they first gave us *The Sun Also Rises* to read in eighth grade, no one new it was about impotence," he said. "I just thought he and that nurse couldn't be together because they were not suited for one another."

"Well, maybe the impotence is a symbolism for something else. You know, the Lost Generation and all that shit," I said.

Stevie asked, "You really think *The Old Man and the Sea* is about dicks?"

"It can be about a lot of things. There are other interpretations. But yeah, on some level."

Nevertheless, impotence is among those concepts which people should stop sexualizing, along with breasts and vaginas and women in general. Impotence is powerlessness; powerlessness is limiting, limiting is random: noun, noun, adjective, adjective.

Rowing, rowing forward, back and forth, through the sea of words, and realizing the tides have changed, and you can't control the tides and you'll flounder in a shipwreck: perhaps sink your boat and drown. Boats; drowning—what a violation of nature! But we created boats, so we must be violations of nature as well.

When you think about it, everything violates nature—that's why there are so many things extinct and so many wars and nuclear programs and global warming. There is a beach in Rio de Janeiro where my husband and I have visited, and it is right next to the nuclear plant. They call it the Plant Beach. On our last trip there, we passed it while doing some exploring; the locals told us that beach was perfectly fine for swimming. The locals—I am Brazilian, still I refer to Brazilians as the locals. Well, I guess I'm not American, either even though I moved here at the prosperous age of twelve—just the perfect foreigner, with no accent and an anonymous brow.

Anyway, a couple of months later, we found out there had been a small leak on the Plant, nothing the country should be worried about, yet something frequent beach-goers were right to lose their minds over—the way things are going in the world, I'm sure one of these says my husband will catch a radioactive sardine, and have the government tell him to replace his regular spot for the artificial waters of a pool with waves; all climates and natural habitats reconstructed for the pleasure of your and the fish.

And the pool of fish will be so extensive he will barely notice the difference.

And we'll keep building this world of ours on top of all other worlds, and we'll believe in it vehemently, in the alphabet and its sounds and its trackless trains of thought. The trains we have built ourselves; they travel farther and further away from nature into reality And it would all be alright, you know; had words no say in it.

* * *

For a while I was a translator, from English to Greek to Ancient Greek to English. By the time you got back to English, you had something completely different from the original. Translation is an art of the devil. All words have their own unbreakable self, which one is not to interfere with. Somewhere in a dictionary all of these words that mean the same, but not quite the same, you see—all of them are fighting in different languages.

But I am over translation and these words that have their own very busy lives and never have time for your questions. From now on, I'll do no explaining—I'll just state facts.

My favorite living soul is a poodle named Harlow. That may seem rather cold to you, but it's the truth, and the coldest thing in the world is hypocrisy in my view. Harlow often sniggles up on my lap; he is here right now as I write these passages in my diary. I'm writing this because my therapist told me it would be good, to get things out of my system. She does not understand there is nothing to purge, not one thing, and that is specifically the problem.

Therapists always think there's something hiding underneath. But there's nothing but words underneath. The subconscious is not something to be uncovered because it doesn't exist. The minute you try to pull the blanket on a person, you will realize you are simply skinning them. And you leave them worse off than you found them, thinking there's something wrong so wrong with their ids that they want to have sex with their parents.

Is the sea in Hemingway a representation of the subconscious? Maybe, but maybe it's exactly the opposite (that's the trouble with opposites; they are always symmetrical between themselves, like—2 and 2, which in the end are both the same quality).

156

Maybe the sea is, then, simply the lack of it, the lack of an explanation. Just a deep empty surface that fails to give us answers: we feel powerlessness, as opposed to impotence; resignation.

* * *

If you want to get to the heart of it, good luck. A heart is a functioning organ in a system, and it can only be approached in relationship to the other organs. They say you have to dig through the fat to get to the point, but the fat is as much part of the point as anything else. Sometimes, fat is all there is, and you never get to the point.

I don't believe in psychology; the only reason I have therapy is because all women my age do, and if I didn't, they'd find my weird; like maybe I had something to hide. Obsessively dwelling in oneself and one's motives has been a consistently fashionable thing to do lately. They bever seem to get to the point of realizing that maybe it's actions that create motives, justifications, or than an action is motivated by the meaning it conveys relating to its cause, rather than but the cause itself. Instead, it's just endless masturbation:

Why do you think you do this (talk pompously)? Because I'm too eager to provide I'm different from the other trophy wives. But why? I don't know, I guess I don't consider this position worthy of me. Then why did you put yourself in this position? Because I had to. Or maybe…I'm just throwing this idea in the mix…You feel guilty about marrying a man you don't love when you had other options.

Yes, maybe that is true. Or maybe, I just put myself in this position because I really actually had to, considering my immigration status. And maybe I'm proud of not letting myself be guided by sentimental nonsense, and I like the fact that I don't love him, and I like the fact that I am a reasonable person, and I like reiterating this fact to people. I consciously came up with this characteristic in order to differentiate myself from others. Clara, the rational woman. Clara, the academic. Clara, who has her life all figured out. Clara, the trophy wife who didn't have to be a trophy wife, thus defying the entire trophy wife establishment. That position is not worthy of me, and I want people to know it. But that is exactly why I love this position because I sound so much better than I am compared to everyone else. So what? This is just something else I like about myself, knowing I possess the fatal flaw of vanity like all epic heroes. Now, I have something to define myself by—vain, intelligent, tramp. I'm not so blurry after all in the whole of things.

In the end, all of these justifications, they're just a side-effect from boredom and uncertainty. Psychology, too. When we were cavemen, no one worried about this shit.

We do what we do and come up with reasons afterward; reasons that suit the same old narrative we have for ourselves ever since we as children realized we were alone in this thing. It's all about the narrative I choose to tell, while I, as narrator, observe the I, as character, and omniscient of my world as she is, readily points out every irony in my being.

Growing up has been to me, ever since I turned eighteen, a ridiculous construction. Especially because I don't see any continuity in these histories that are expected to compose my ever-changing cells creating the illusion of myself. None of my cells are the same as they were at birth. I guess I am at least somewhat of a hypocrite. I wonder if, when one is clear minded enough to realize one's a hypocrite, it ceases to be hypocrisy.

We are in a loop as a society. After both World Wars, when things stopped making sense, poor old Earth has been facing an identity crisis, like an awkward teenager who becomes self-destructive. Well, we were already self-destructive. But that's just because we're not natural.

To think we are moving forward and that there is a path for us seems to me absurd. There is no such thing as forward, you see, just as there is no such thing as right and left. When I was a child, I had great difficulty comprehending this; that right and left could change depending on one's position. Tell me, then, where forward is.

Are we getting better? I don't think we're getting better. From the discovery of fire to the invention of the written word, to the first of us to have homes, to Gods, to Reason, to Freedom—I wonder whether we were not all better off as monkeys. But then, there's this human, abhorrently human narrative, with a beginning and a middle and an ending. I wish we'd stop putting thing chronological order.

If, however, moving in some general direction is not human nature, then what caused us to be so obsessed with being fully developed individuals? What has caused us to abandon the generic in favor of the ardently persona? What ailment has caused us to write novels and practice atheism and feel incomplete if we were fine before?

Yet, we are hardly more evolved than people two hundred years ago. Natural selection hadn't then been unceremoniously impeded by our vaccines; we were stronger and less doubtful then. Kids went straight to adulthood without that cursed adolescence. But we were also more prejudiced and ignorant although, the reason for our prejudices was still our thinking we were more evolved than some others.

* * *

I think people are good; that's not the problem. By themselves, people are good, when they are lonely and by themselves. The day we found Harlow, we heard a cry coming from the gate, and there it was, a disheveled poodle, abandoned and panting.

We took him to the vet, who told us he'd probably been kicked multiple times, Ye, I am aware that my argument was that people ae good, but I'm getting there, don't worry.

So, we took the poor dog in, gave him all sorts of medicine, got rid of his flees and balls. Once the neighborhood heard what we'd done, everyone came over to tell us how great it was that we'd taken him in because he'd been wandering around for a while, and they had been feeding him and nurturing him, but none of them could take him in. They'd been very worried when the dog disappeared for a few days; they thought he'd been run over or gotten lost. One of the men who'd been caring for him, upon seeing him again, let out a joyous sigh of relief, and for the first time in a long time, I saw on someone's face an expression of pure happiness. Pure, disinterested happiness.

It's when people are in groups that they do terrible things because they forget who they are. They are no longer people, you see.

But then I wonder why I, so alone, would fall victim to the same disorder.

Although, maybe, I'm like a sponge, forever absorbing the mood of the people around me, a stranger to individuality. The more I think about it, the more I'm convinced that we are defined not by what we are, but what we are not. We need to stop trying to define things by what they are—they're just a mass of vague everything. In the vague everything, one must guide oneself. Lost in a desert of vast

159

impenetrability; the outside so much greater than you and the beautifully vertical vastness of your own desert, you will never be able to fill the world with yourself again. You're outside the self, in exile. I, in fact, can't remember a time I wasn't in exile.

My therapist tells me the reason why I'm disenchanted has nothing to do with this unfortunate world, but with my general lack of activity. She sent me to a soup kitchen. I went there for two days, then decided to establish a soup kitchen of my own just so I wouldn't have to work there. I donated a bunch of money to charities helping Syria and Syrians in Syria and in here and Germany. But I would never be strong enough to actually do something, rather than pay for it. I think that says way too much about me. If I ever got involved in sensitive issues, I would sooner or later be broken. Is it because I'm rick, and I think I'm made of crystal? But I wasn't born rich. I wasn't born anything. Thank God I have money now; money can really make a difference.

It's not so much that I must make my life worthwhile because that would be selfish. I hate those people who only do good things in order to be considered good people. That's not how it works. No one gets it; that's not how it works.

I am but a fallacy. I waste my time with words. Still, words are the only thing I have. They are the only ones that seem to pierce through the stubborn texture of reality, however twisted in meaning, however literal the translation.

Words are building this world and it will exist so long as I keep writing them down, and then it will be forgotten about until someone decides to read it. But right now, at this moment, as you're reading this, I still exist, and that's enough for me.

GODDESS

ASHLEY MARIE EGAN

My body is
my home—
a universe
wrapped in
skin and bone,
a star map of
scars and moles,
a beautiful temple
you cannot own.

I AM BECOME THE WESTERN HEMLOCK

ABIGAIL ECKSTINE

I am at my largest
Full strength of soul
Have come into being
Not like flowers—I have nothing against their fragile petals
But my strength
Is more than a tree

I am no longer small
Not anyone's little peach
I am done with being
Just a fruit on a limb
By righteous power
I have become god
Not to have power over others
But only over me.

PEAR RUST

SUZY EYNON

Fallen pears dotted the August-dry lawn. Daisy counted ten this time, most with bites taken by neighborhood rabbits or smaller nibbles from the rats. She picked up dropped pears every day in this stretch of summer bleeding into fall, each fruit sighing a heavy *thump* as it hit the crispy grass. She never ate the fruit herself because it was woody, inedible. She'd asked around at farmers markets, and a vender once told her to refrigerate the crop for weeks before trying to eat them, but she didn't have enough space to chill dozens of pears. She didn't ask for the tree, it was already in the front yard when she moved into the house.

The tree itself was afflicted with pear rust, a pervasive fungus of the Pacific Northwest. Daisy came from a desert, and her introduction to the Pacific Northwest included ailments new to her, both in her body and all around: eczema on her hands after handling yard leaves which left itchy gashes on her palms, all manner of mosses and molds bursting from trees and corners and holes. A green layer on everything until what existed beneath rotted and crumbled. The first time she noticed the rust, she was repulsed. The fungus clung to the tree's leaves in spikes, like a cluster of horns. She'd read that the pear rust also sought host in conifers or junipers, bursting from the leaves of these trees before jumping to a pear tree. Just hopping back and forth between hosts, a greedy guest slowly blemishing all surfaces.

Daisy began her walk to the pharmacy. She needed to get there today, because Petey had taken his last dose this morning, and she'd already postponed this walk by a day because she hadn't felt well. She realized after she pulled the front door shut that she would have to walk at a fast pace to get to the pharmacy before they temporarily closed for lunch. She thought ahead to a scenario in which she arrived just as they pulled the shutters down in front of the register and she had to wait in a pressed plastic seat until they returned. She tried to walk as fast as she could.

Some days she felt her body moving through gelatin while other days she moved with less effort. Her period had finally arrived after disappearing for two months. She was relieved and not when it showed up again. She'd assumed it was menopause come early, which made her feel a sense of loss – of youth, of potential to someday have a child – but she also felt tired and ready to slide into acceptance. Sometimes her lower extremities felt filled with rocks, and that's how she pictured them, as bags filled with pebbles.

Today, pain radiated from her low back down the reverse of her legs, so that she felt she expended a lot of effort just to keep her sneakers moving over the pavement. Her right sneaker felt loose so that her foot swam around inside, rubbing and pressing, but she couldn't afford the time to bend over and re-tie it, so she altered her stride to put less pressure on that foot.

The sun emerged from behind the clouds and sweat threatened to bloom in her armpits and under her breasts which today weren't contained enough by her gray sports bra. Daisy considered pulling her sweatshirt off, but she didn't have time to stop, and she preferred to sweat under the extra layer in exchange for keeping it on as a buffer between herself and the world. Her discomfort could be measured and categorized and then ignored accordingly, and the overheated feeling was less a threat than her need to hide herself. She checked her phone for the time. She needed to keep going.

She rounded the corner in front of the pharmacy and followed the walkway, scanning like a hunted animal for any vehicles on their path to run her down. She slipped a mask from her sweatshirt pocket and looped it around her ears before entering through the automatic door. She spotted the neon Pharmacy signage at the back of the store, and quickened her pace, noticing first a closed shutter—*oh no, she was too late*—then glancing to the right and seeing the open windows for prescription pick up.

The woman in front of her finished up with the pharmacist. "We don't have it, and we can't tell you who might have it," the pharmacist said.

"What about in Lynnwood?" the woman asked. "Do you think they have it?" She scrolled through her phone.

164

"They're out of it everywhere, so I would suggest calling the doctor—"

"I'm going to go use the bathroom, and when I come back, I have more questions." The woman walked away.

"You," the pharmacist said to Daisy. "Picking up? Your name?"

"Well, my name is Daisy Henderson, but the prescription is for a cat. Petey? Henderson," Daisy said. She pulled a cat-head-shaped wallet from her tote bag.

"Oh, yes," the pharmacist said. She stepped away and returned waving a white baggy. "Address?"

Daisy recited her address.

"For...Peter CAT Henderson?" the pharmacist repeated, as if Cat was his middle name.

Daisy blushed. "Yes, that's him." She didn't correct the pharmacist. His middle name was actually Kyle.

"Okay, $114.97."

"What?" Daisy said. "Oh! Oh. That's...wow. That's a lot."

The pharmacist wasn't unkind. "Did you get it somewhere else before?"

Daisy confirmed, yes. "It was like $10 last time."

"Maybe it was for a smaller dose? This is for 75mg."

"Maybe," Daisy said, though she knew it was the same strength she got last time. She didn't know what to do. She knew the medicine was a common human one, an inexpensive one even, not like the costly cat chemo he took several times a week. But anything she could do to prolong his life, to extend his existence in parallel to hers, she would do. She knew, too, that some didn't do this for pets. Couldn't, or wouldn't. It felt such a struggle just to get the refill called in, to leave the house, to journey over land to obtain these expensive heart pills. "It's okay. He needs it, so." She produced her credit card as digits swirled in her head.

"Sorry," the pharmacist whispered as she handed Daisy the receipt.

Daisy was distracted as she crossed the parking lot, dodging cars waiting to pull from spaces or turn into the lot. Maybe she'd asked the vet for the wrong medication refill. Or maybe the old pharmacy erroneously put the cat's medication through Daisy's insurance. She swallowed a rising sense that she'd been taken advantage of in some way she wasn't able to place but which still upset her.

She pressed the crosswalk button with a crooked pinky then wiped her soiled fingertip against her too-heavy sweatshirt. She squeezed the remaining drop of hand sanitizer into her palm. The light changed and the walk button blinked, so she threw the empty bottle into her bag and started to cross. She watched as a boat of a car headed her direction, golden and shining as it turned over the crosswalk. It approached but didn't stop until its front bumper was within a foot of kissing her knees. Maybe the driver thought Daisy didn't deserve to cross since she hadn't immediately leapt into the crosswalk when the light changed, or thought Daisy moved too slowly.

Daisy kept walking but looked back to glare at the woman behind the wheel. She didn't say a word or lift a finger in salute, she just stared at the driver, and the driver stared back. They held each other's gaze until Daisy reached the other side.

Once she was out of range of the crosswalk, Daisy started to cry. She didn't like to brag, as a rule, but her public displays of tears were controlled, undetected. She could cry without making a sound. She looked around to make sure she wasn't in anyone's way before she paused on the sidewalk. She caught portions of conversation from two men in a nearby lot. One said to the other, "…and he said, hey I'm vaccinated, and the other guy just started punching…" Daisy pulled her mask from her face and dropped it into her bag.

Daisy used a neighborhood shortcut. She just wanted to be inside her house, where her cat rested, just the two of them. As she cut past a neighbor's house, she imagined a scenario in which he said something to her about cutting through this street, like what if he asked her if she lived here and what she was doing. She preemptively imagined herself responding, *I live on the other street.*

She cut across her front lawn, and again she noticed the fallen pears. She knew she should pick them up and throw them in the compost bin before they enticed rats. Before the neighbors noticed how many littered the lawn, whichever arbitrary number of pears was too many to leave to rot in daylight for passersby to see. *Such a waste. I wasn't sure if you were going to pick those this year.* She kicked a pear from her footpath. She looked forward to the fall, when the fruit would stop coming in and she would no longer have to clean up after it, when the cold would freeze out the bearing of fruit for another year.

BRUISED ORANGES

KRIS HILES

We are made to carry,
starting with toys, expectations growing
with larger hands, longer arms,
longer legs. Are we closer to God
when we carry something?

The sky on our shoulders settles
as our movement slows, settles on us,
knickknacks and dolls,
filled with potential. The tap runs
constantly. We expect hands
to steady us in a tornado. Hands
give us a storm to bear—
we cannot take the sky
and cram it into a teapot.

Someday, we all grow
into universes, paralleled
in makeup mirrors. We contain
infinite reflections, the weight of lead,
and tales we tell in passing. Notions
of wonder, silver-plated passions
for handmade jewelry and photography.

Even painted,
we cannot maintain
the appearance of angels when we juggle
like clowns. We trip over our shoes—
we are so full, our small hands
cannot carry each other so well, anymore.

MOUNTAINS, MUSTARD SEEDS
AND MARIGOLDS

JASMIN LANKFORD

When a woman has a miscarriage,
it's tradition for other women to offer her
forget-me-not flower seeds

in memory of the child. My friends give me
mustard seeds so I don't forget my faith.
I haven't been able to move my mountain.

I am a graveyard. I am a summer beach house
in the winter. My womb carries the wound.
My friends ask me if I want to bury the seeds,

but part of me doesn't want the risk of another wilt.
Every summer season, I prepare myself for the pruning.
I look to marigold flowers in my mourning,

how their golden blossoms guide the lost home.
My friends say: home has never left you.
All flowers need the soil and its nutrients to survive.

They remind me to stay rooted, keep the mustard seeds close.
When they ask me to deadhead the flowers fading out of bloom
to foster fresh growth, I tell them: I am not a garden anymore.

WHAT MY MOTHER COULDN'T TEACH ME

KAYLA KING

I already said too much. Yet, I prefer
the swish, the snip, sinking sharp teeth
to the thin sheaf of each page.

Don't leave the house, she reminded before
the days and the honey, the coffee
and the plums and the pieces of peppermint gum,

and yes, the boxes of matches
also emptied in that time.
So I didn't go.

Now, these paper flowers find life
in champagne flutes. Grown from my hands
and my time and my inability to inherit my mother's gift

for tedium. She was always better at collecting
seeds, praying to sky and sun to soak the empty beds
and hope for something. Such a belief daunts my days.

Even here. But perhaps I will unveil my work to the world
if my mother refuses an exegesis of every flower
she's ever grown, words punctuated and lacking

parentage for me. But this is the cost
of blooming, of planting yourself
out of reach

and promising,
I'll be good; I'll be better
when this ends.

FOR BODY, FOR MIND

CHRISTY NOLAN

IX

Her fingertip follows a sole stretch of skin,
a dip from the pale,
once plum, now peach,
nesting the rim below her navel.
Her index, bit to blood, burrows before pulling back.
She can't bring herself to try the cold of cocoa butter;
studying the mirror more, now, to see if she's mourned yet.

VIII

Ten days pre-pandemic she put it all on her left wrist.
Two lines bloomed twin scars;
one for body, one for mind that took form
in the film of reflection. Poorly healed and patchy.

VII

She grew in a home that sheltered the unborn
and prepared her to pick at the leftover
deli meat from forgotten
lunches; co-parented
by the spare rosary next to the table.

VI

Her memories of motherhood,
defined by the distress of a team
trying their best. Medical bills and bike rides,
knocks on the master door,
never needing to worry for her sake.

V

The women before her would mock such shallow words,
nurtured with guilt. Her bones had not earned bliss back,
and uptight impulse was no home for new minds.

IV

She had the thought before pink plastic, bitter
in her grip, and settled on harvesting sanity
from a formula of sleeping pills and advice to others
long before she could look them in the eye. It was enough
to resemble adult.

III

Forgiveness won't be found in a flush
and few hours faced forward
from a couch borrowed
for the weekend.

II

And relief is a tremor held tight
by home, which lies
in the palm of a man with three months 'stubble,
morning breath, and a light in his gaze too bright
for the sake of sunrise.

I

There's a name in her phone seven dusks
from today; and it's aged since she saved it,
filling space, shedding seconds. Former tics
swim to surface, breaking up mind's crusade:
Roll wrists. Crack knuckles. Stiff shoulders.
Release.

THE HOME

MANJUSHA HARI

Me, a bare whirlwind
aimless, yet stubborn!
I never touch
the shoreline or the sand hills.
I never taste
the wordings of pleasure.
I thawed, I trampled,
I shattered, and I divided…
The tough silence
seeding in the womb of my thoughts.
Still the last drops of laugh remains
in the name of your hoar love!
We drift apart
like a scattered metaphor…
and the time hanging
on my untied hair as the bud sentience!
Gift me fetters
and let me break it.
Let me reborn
in the painless frigidity, with you.
But the waves of air encaging me,
in the illusion of lost souls!
I'm a distressing whirlwind
which you never expected.
Not the land, not the sea,
not the hills or not the hearts
I belong to the trench of hell!

THE WOMB, OR "WHY PREGNANT WOMEN RUB THEIR BELLIES"

ANNIE MARHEFKA

my belly is a den
I feel my cub push down, down
towards the mouth of the cave and I whisper
not yet, not yet, little bear

the tummy is a fishbowl
I must guzzle enough water
to keep its insides sloshing with
amniotic fluid and baby limbs

my abdomen is a nest of braided twigs
gathered from the woods of my
mistakes and yet I build it
stronger still

the stomach is a web
where I've spun up my sack of
placenta and cord and body and I hope
that the wind won't blow through its silks

my womb is a pit dug in the sand and like
the turtle's flippers smoothing the grains,
I softly pat the outer skin of
my little one's home

TROPHIES

DW MCKINNEY

The thief flees the homestead with the contents of the woman's bedroom and half of her kitchen. She chases after the thief but loses him in the woods when he hides in a cave.

The thief finds comfort with his stolen possessions. They're his trophies. The more he has, the more he believes he's winning. Though what the contest is, he can't say for sure.

While the thief waits for the woman to forget that he's taken her rosebush, the knobs from her cabinets, and a case of wine, he converts the cave into a home. He drags in moss-covered logs from the woods and calls them chairs. He hangs silk bedsheets across the cave entrance.

Bored, the thief roams the woods, and he stumbles upon a black bear bathing in a river.

"I could use an exotic pet," he says. "Or a beast to protect my belongings."

Hearing this, the bear turns around. "Do I know you?" it grumbles.

"I was just admiring your hide," the thief says.

"I keep a modest hygiene regimen," the bear huffs. "You know what they say about cleanliness…"

"It's next to godliness."

"No," says the bear. "It reveals our better natures."

"Ah! A creature of purpose. A lover of respectable proclivities! We'll get along well," exclaims the thief. He invites the bear to his cave. He leads it away from a trail, just in case the woman is still searching for him.

At the cave, the thief throws a lavish candlelit party. He and the bear eat stale rye bread on the woman's fine china set. The thief opens the case of wine and takes a bottle for himself and one for the bear. They toast to new friendships and reflect on their lives.

Three bottles in and spittle flies from their mouths as they roar and scream. The thief rips the bedsheets. The bear gnaws on an ottoman-tree stump. The sound of their raucous good time echoes through the woods and catches the attention of the determined woman still searching for the thief.

When the thief awakens from his drunken stupor, he spies the bear tiptoeing away. "Please don't go," the thief begs.

"I was not myself last night," the bear says. "I have responsibilities waiting for me."

"Then let us create a new memory of more civilized behavior." The thief opens the remaining bottles of wine. He and the bear toast to newer friendships. They toast to better times. They toast to comfort, and they toast to dignity until the bear passes out.

The thief eyes the bear. He imagines what it must be like to be such a magnificent creature, to have such luxurious black fur. *This, too, must be a form of winning*, he thinks.

He shaves the bear and fashions a suit from the fur. Then he lays the woman's velvet robe over the naked beast.

Never let it be said that I took advantage of another, he thinks.

At nightfall, the thief slips into the woods. He caresses his fur, admiring its luster though it is patchy in some spots. He believes that to wear the bear is to be the bear. He is certain that his eyesight is sharper now, his hearing exceptional. The thief chuckles to himself.

He is finally the best he will ever be.

The thief bends to the ground and walks on all fours. He thinks about the wine-drunk bear and imitates the damp roar that delighted him the night before. It reverberates through the trees, and he is certain the stars shine brighter for him now. The thief arches his back and grumbles. He stomps and scratches the trees, then he ambles toward the river where he first met the bear.

Sitting on a rock, he gazes at the moon and splashes the rushing water. He sees two small cubs wandering in a meadow across the river. Their cries for "Mama" upset him. He tut-tuts at their squeaking and shakes his head.

"It's a shame they have no one to look after them," he says. The thief then strokes the folds of his fur, gets up, and heads home.

When he returns to the cave, it is empty except for the woman awaiting him. She raises her shotgun.

"Wait!" the thief cries. "I'm not what you think I am!"

"You're exactly what I think you are," the woman says. "And you'll make a fine trophy for my wall." She aims and shoots.

Across the river a hairless bear does not pause at the sound of gunfire. Its limbs carry candlesticks, chipped plates, a half-full bottle of wine. The velvet robe blows open as it reunites with its hungry cubs.

THE YEAR OF THE SUMMER ROBE

MOLLY GREER

My winter robe kept me warm
through the year of hibernation—

The year when we bathed
ourselves in artificial light
and watched the people
became numbers and the numbers
lose all meaning.

Technicolor tally boxes
going up,   up,   up—
Blood donations to the cause
of personal freedom.

But this is the year of the summer robe—

And my braless, lumpy body looks elegant
draped in sky blue imitation silk,
adorned with painted birds and blossoms.

I feel like I should go do something
when I'm in my summer robe,
but gliding through the kitchen is enough—
skirt tails flapping at my heels,
bird mug and watering can in hand.

I float out into the summer heat
and down to the garden,
where I water my seeds
and try to remember
what it feels like to watch things grow.

THE WISH

MARIA URIARTE TORRONTEGUI

Your hair falls down your shoulders
Black and bright.
A bulb could not blind me better.
I breathe in and I stop the world.
I'm all ears, honey. What do you want?
Now, only you can count on me.
I've never been much of a talker or a hero,
But just say it, and all that, I can be.

When you talk, you're a God,
You don't need anyone.
It's six o'clock, time to leave,
But I wish you would spend five more minutes
Explaining to me how blue birds will be
When they're grown,
And how the pink worms in their beaks won't be free.
You'd say "it's just biology,"
While alone in the room where we used to meet
Back when we didn't know each other,
And anyone from the outside could see
Through those library windows
That we were just working.

I forgot my pen on the table on purpose.
Please, remind me I did it
And I won't write about anything else
Ever again, I promise.

I love afternoons when they last.
Hope won't leave me, it's hellish, like pain.
Some days I wonder if they might be the same
Twins with identical genes, different parents and pets.
Different, too, their notebooks and pen names.
One smiles at the sun at sunrise,

The other waves at the moon at sunset.

I watch them both and I listen to all
The waves howling for help.
I let them be and I crawl to the sand
When beauty leaves the beach.
But I am lucky, I don't need the stars
Or the satellites.
It's enough with the in between,
No days or nights.

I'll eat the shells,
Drink the seagull's scratched ocean
So you live, and I'll be
The one you won't notice,
Because with you by my side
Beauty never leaves me,
Not even in a starless desert.

BROWN ROSES

JASMIN LANKFORD

I'll rebirth my brown baby as a rose.
Bathed in soil at a spot baked with light,
I'll water with salty tears as she grows.
I'll rebirth my brown baby as a rose.

See her bloom and forget feeling lows,
Stop wanting to die to see her in sight.
I'll rebirth my brown baby as a rose,
Bathed in soil at a spot baked with light.

PANSIES & CUCUMBERS

KRIS HILES

One of the nurses laughs,
the other knows sea water.

Where is the doctor
my mother cries, and when can we see
what is going to happen?

She is behind me
at this first moment of breathing,
bleeding and preserving the walls of our house –
she will tell me later how the windows shook,
how I was born with strength
to raise more than gardens.

We are gifted
with incomprehensible prophecy. I fall in love
with the legend
of Cassandra, with my mother
crying in the sun, planting pansies and cucumbers.

A garden rises,
lives – it does not return.

Where is the doctor
my mother cries, and when can we see
what is going to happen?

I only return to stand behind her
at her last moment of breathing. When I scream
the windows do not shake, and I know
her power is not mine.

What is going to happen? I know
laughter and sea water
and nothing but questions.

MARTINI GLASS MEMOIRS

JASMIN LANKFORD

We have a dead baby together.
She's the size of a green olive.
These days, I drink up.

AFTER YOUR AFTERWARD, I FIND MY GOING FORWARD

RONDA PISZK BROATCH

Inky is first month of every journal I've ever.
Brief. Wintered. Inventoried. So you wrote
and mostly didn't. On my wall sings the cow

skull, early gift to myself after your after-
birthday death. Sorrow lives inside it, a history
of air and absence, landscape of bone

and suture. When balled up my paper skin
is intimate with itself. Because you task me,
Mother, with lists, I turn out my pockets. Because

you chore me, I run in circles. Because. You.
I am always the one who remembers how
sun becomes a chain link fence against

the walls and windows, you are always the one
to pull me from it's much-too-brightness. Yes.
My grandfather visits with asbestos omens.

My grandmother visits with prescient papers
and an embrace. How like her! How like
the whale to swallow us into its sanctuary

of lost and found faith, those twins
inseparable. We are heading into the ink
of black holes, into the Year of the Return

of Wisdom, into the sweetness of the never-plan,
Beloved Remembrance, Mistaken Otherwise.

ONCE HEARD FROM A PSYCHIC IN THE YEARS BEFORE

KAYLA KING

Something secret settles gossamer
against your ankle. It must be accuracy
of divination from a decade ago, softer
than the words your mother spoke
six years yesterday.

You looked at a house today
with three bedrooms. And the space hums
like a sepulcher ready to suck everything
in with a ping.

There is only you.

Sprawl in the tall grass outside. Hold two stones
to the skin of your stomach, and ask
what now? It was supposed to be the year
of the twins, and you find the world begging
you to pick apart and reassemble
like the bones of birds strung up with silk ties
in your grandfather's study.

Keep two candlesticks
lit in front of the window as an imitation.

But no, that's not right. Recall the psychic
mentioning that what she meant
was you must eat two cakes to yourself
to celebrate empty shells waiting
to be filled.

No longer fear losing yourself,
only the inability to incant the infertile soil beyond
the garden's gate to give you milkweed and thistle
and thyme. How much of this belief

comes from the curve of the moon
in that card you framed by your bedside?

It looked full once, and you obsess over the wane
of waiting. Uncertainty snatches at you
without speaking to the shuttered suffering of being
so old in this lifetime,

knowing too much of the sick spin
from winding up a staircase in the belly
of a lighthouse.

Better than a whale, someone else might say,
noting the creature on the shelf.
But you didn't shape it the way you would've liked.
It's only an inheritance meant to remind you
of your ancestors

acting like a heart could be tossed back
out to sea.

Don't you see?

The world is just the same if you can't
replicate. And this is only another year,
ordinary in its oath to move on
without permission. In a few hours
this will be yesterday, and you won't care
how this ends.

ULTRASOUND

JGEORGE

The nurse calls me in for the scan and wonders aloud,
whether I am pregnant
Only if she saw how the ultrasound enlarged on the screen
projecting my swollen ovaries like elongated balloons
in black and white,
pregnant with bead like cysts of its own rimming the outer edges.
Those tiny millimeter length pouches that conspired,
rebelled against my will,
ceasing my choice of getting pregnant any sooner any easier,
baptizing a new condition on me—a syndrome of polycystic ovaries.
Then it was the doctor's turn with his small conversation,
To ease my unexpected flash blindness, the deafness of a whiplash
he needs to know whether I'm married whether my husband
is urging for a baby,
forgetting the ultrasound was about me and my unformed babies.

SISTERS IN EXILE

BETTY J. COTTER

The first time Alice slips away, she knows she will pay for it. But as the sun slants into the back windows this July morning of 1947, she feels the tug of the ocean. It's barely eight o'clock. The girls are already on the bus to day camp, Johnny dozes in his crib, and Jim is going out back to paint a vacant cabin. She waits until he disappears, then runs out through the motel office before someone can stop her.

Only after crossing Route 1, walking a block, and slipping behind a row of gas stations, stores, and restaurants does she slow down. There it looms, right on the water: the shell of a new motel. It will be 32 units, Jim says, nearly twice as large as their Pink Azalea Courts, and it will have a pool. As soon as he heard this, he called up an excavating company and began digging a hole. If we don't have a swimming pool, too, we will go out of business, he says.

Banging nails, two men balance on the rafters. The Surfside Motor Inn—that is the name on the temporary sign—will open in October, near Alice's due date. Rubbing out a stitch in her side, she stops to watch the men, shirtless, perched on the roof peak. They are lean and tanned. Though she stands there several minutes, watching them jostle beams into place and swing their hammers, they don't look down or wave.

Through the next vacant lot, she reaches the beach. Back home, in Rhode Island, the soft, sloping dunes give a *sssfft* sound as you step. The Florida sands grind beneath your soles like sugar spilled on a hardwood floor. She hurries across their wide expanse to the waves. As far as the eye can see, from the shore to sea to horizon, all is flat.

How long has it been since her feet touched Rhode Island sand? Almost a year, when her sister Lenore married. And how much has changed in those 12 months? Daddy, dropping dead in the potato

189

fields. Mother, leaving the farm, abandoning it really, the way one might ditch a car whose engine has stopped working.

Last summer, Alice took for granted they would return every year with the children. But Jim has no interest in going home, and the farm is vacant, the house locked up. Mother has bought a new house in town with Daddy's life insurance. And here Alice is pregnant again, just three months after Johnny's birth last October. Seven months along now, she feels ill almost constantly. That shift, when morning sickness fades and a glorious feeling of well-being descends, hasn't happened this time. Instead, she dizzies easily, and can hardly stomach more than a few bites.

It shouldn't be this way.

Alice reaches the water's edge. The waves roar and retreat, drowning out the carpenters' hammers. How wonderful to be here, on the beach, alone! For a moment she can almost pretend to be on the rocky edge of Watch Hill, examining the breakers foam against the endless spit of Napatree Point. She can forget the motel, Jim's ill humor, the children's incessant demands. No one checking in or checking out, no one complaining that a room isn't clean or the towels are too thin. Out of reach of the children, particularly Johnny, who seems to need her every minute, not like the girls at all.

She leans against a piling, an old telephone pole someone has buried in the sand, and clasps her hands across her belly. She cannot wait to be rid of this baby. Yes—that is how she thinks of it—that moment of expulsion, that final push when all you can think is: *Get out. Get out of me.* She told Jim she didn't want any more children. The girls, now 5 and 7, just reached a manageable age when Johnny was born. They must do something—be more careful—but he refuses to wear a safety, and he wouldn't let her use a diaphragm. She visited a doctor and got one anyway but could never be sure she was using it correctly. Well, now she knows.

Mother simply stopped sleeping with Daddy. She kicked him out of their bedroom and relegated him to the den. Even as a girl about Darcy's age, Alice knew that wasn't right. She and Meredith and Lenore slept in one room upstairs, and Alice coveted that narrow den, imagining lining the window ledge with seashells and tacking her sketches on the wall. But she could never suggest it. Daddy wasn't thrown out of Mother's bed temporarily; he was exiled.

And to Florida she was exiled and in Florida she will stay. Like a flamingo, Alice raises one foot up and tucks it behind the other knee. She is becoming one, a fat pink body with two stick legs. Just a plastic lawn ornament, somebody's decoration, forever trapped in a place where she doesn't belong. While the home she loves, the farm, her sisters, her mother, all have vanished, far over the blue horizon.

"Where have you been?" Jim glares from behind the office counter. His face is flushed and tight.

In the corner, Johnny lies on the floor, trying to roll over.

"I had to do all the checkouts," he says, not waiting for an answer. "The telephone keeps ringing. I didn't get one wall painted before the couple in 3C came looking for me. Said they'd rung the bell a dozen times."

It is probably obvious where she's been. Her hair, tangled and salty, hangs over her eyes. She has tracked sand on the worn carpet.

"I thought you were sick," he goes on. "I tore through the apartment. Then the sisters checking out of Cabin 5 said they saw you crossing the street."

So, the worry and concern gave way to rage early on. Her head slightly bowed, she stands and takes his tirade, like a disobedient child.

"You left the baby. He was screaming in his crib. How could you do such a thing? He was wet clear through."

"I want to go home, Jim."

He seems not to have heard. "Get yourself cleaned up, for heaven's sake, so I can get back to work."

"I mean it. I don't want to have this baby down here." She adds the "down here" only for effect. She wants to put the period after "baby."

"We've been over this." He leans down and picks up Johnny, holding him out toward her. "I have too much to do this summer to go traipsing up north."

"I don't mean a vacation." She keeps her arms folded, refusing to take the baby. "I want to go home."

"You mean permanently?" He sounds incredulous, as though she's suggested moving to Greenland. "You can't be serious."

"We have no family here. Even in the slow season you're working yourself to death. It's ungodly hot all the time. I miss my

191

mother."

He gives a little sound in the back of his throat, a sort of "huh," and turns away. He walks through the kitchen into their bedroom, where he slips Johnny into the crib. Johnny grabs the railing, trying to pull himself up, wailing. Alice blocks the doorway.

"Let me through," Jim says. "I have things to do."

"Give me one good reason we should stay here."

"How about the ten thousand we've invested in this place? All the work I've put into it? We'll never get that back."

"We could sell tomorrow. You've said so yourself."

"With a pool out there that's half dug?"

His damned fool idea. Now a dirty hole gapes between the front units and Route 1. Alice rubs her side, trying to catch her breath. "So, we finish the pool."

"Daytona is about to explode, Alice. That's the whole reason I'm building the pool." He speaks with exaggerated slowness. "You don't leave an investment before it pays off."

"We didn't come down here to make money."

His eyes shift away and then back. No longer brown, they are almost black, two pinpricks of dark. The baby stops crying.

"Alice," he says.

Her name is his warning shot. She knows it, she recognizes it, but she ignores it.

"We ran away," she says. "But you can't run forever. Sooner or later you've got to face it."

"There's nothing up there for us! Goddamn it, why can't you understand that?"

They still have two guests, an elderly couple staying the week in Room 6, who usually don't emerge until after 10 o'clock. Even with their door closed they must hear him.

"There's nothing for us here, either." She tries to keep her voice low. "Nothing but this blasted heat and work and—"

It has something to do with what separates them from each other, her loneliness and his detachment. The distance from home—the long, lonely stretch of Route 1, the nautical miles by sea. But the only word she can think of is *shame*, and she cannot say that out loud.

"Listen to me." Jim brushes a hand through his hair as if dislodging something forgotten. "I am not moving back up north. And neither are you. Our life is here now."

"Jim, there's the farm." She knows he doesn't want to hear this. "It's just sitting there. I know we could make a go of it. We'd be back home, with family, to support us, to help us when we needed it."

He makes that sound, "huh," again. "And just how would that work? What family, exactly, did you have in mind? Your mother? Your brother-in-law?" He waves his hand at her as though it holds a dirty handkerchief. She wants to say, "It's all in your head. No one has it in for you," but can't be sure it is true. She keeps quiet.

"I thought so," he says. And at that, she gives up, takes the wailing baby and swings her pregnant body away.

* * *

The next morning, the girls miss the bus to camp. Alice hustles them into the car. Their yellow one-piece rompers are clean but the only towels she can find are two ragged ones from the motel's discard pile. As she drives, the girls chatter in the backseat about the day's planned activity, who excels at this new butterfly stroke, when they will get a field trip. They pet Johnny, who is perched between them in his little red carrier, and wetly kiss his cheeks. At a red light Ellen leans forward and pokes her mother's elbow.

"Mom? Why is that man in uniform?"

Alice looks to where she points, at the corner, where a soldier waits for a bus. "He's from the base."

"What does that mean?"

"The Air Force base," Darcy says importantly. "He's an airman. Right, Mom?"

Alice nods. Ellen leans back, then pipes up again, "I thought the war was over."

"It is, but there are still men in the service."

"Why? We aren't fighting anyone, are we?"

"No," Alice says, looking up briefly at the rear-view mirror, "no, of course we aren't, but we always need some military men to protect us."

But Ellen keeps it up. Would we go to war again? Could Daddy get drafted? Where is his uniform?

"He doesn't still have it," Darcy says. "Nobody keeps a uniform. You have to give it back, so someone else can wear it."

"I don't believe you. I bet that man kept his, and just wears it 'cause he likes to."

"Nobody wears a uniform who doesn't have to."

"Where is it?" Ellen pokes her mother again. "Is it with our winter clothes?"

Alice opens her mouth, tastes a lie, and shuts it again. A bus stops in the right lane, blocking traffic. She is too close to swing out and pass. The boulevard swarms with cars and taxis and these intercity buses; they have widened the road to four lanes but it has only made traffic worse. Where have all these people come from?

"Mom." Ellen raises her voice. "Where is it?"

They are moving again. She signals right.

"Leave her alone, Ellen, she's driving."

"Maybe he has pictures of it," Ellen says. "Let's ask him tonight."

"No," Alice says. She looks in the mirror – Ellen's eyes pop at the vehemence in her mother's voice. Alice looks back at the road just in time to see the back bumper of a cream-colored Oldsmobile. She jams on the brakes.

The steering wheel's hard metal slams against her rib cage, just above her belly. Johnny wails. Ellen, too, starts to cry, claiming she's banged her head on the front seat.

"Johnny's lip is bleeding," Darcy announces.

Only yesterday she wished away this baby she carries. Now Johnny has split his lip, Ellen hurt her head, and Alice nearly flown through the windshield. By some miracle she avoided an accident, missing the Oldsmobile's chrome bumper by inches, but she can't help thinking this close call is her punishment for yesterday.

Ahead of the Olds, on the crosswalk, an old woman, cradling a tiny white poodle, limps across the street. Alice imagines the news story: Daytona woman rear-ends car, which strikes and kills elderly woman.

The Olds driver, a man in a brown fedora, glares back at her and waves his hand wildly out the window, as though to inform onlookers of her ineptitude. For a second Alice fears he might get out, but then the Oldsmobile accelerates. It takes a moment before she can follow, creeping now.

When they reach the YMCA, the blue school bus stands empty

in the far corner of the parking lot. She reaches back to wipe Ellen's smudged cheeks but her daughter sniffles, twists away and yanks the car door open. Darcy has already bolted. As they run down the sidewalk and into the building, Alice climbs into the back seat, takes out a handkerchief and cleans the tears and blood from Johnny's face. He rammed face-first into the car seat's fake steering wheel, but his only injury is the swollen lip.

Her ribs will be sore; Ellen has a bruise on her temple; but no one is seriously hurt, and the car is unscathed. The near miss has been harrowing, but it accomplished one thing: changing the subject.

* * *

Regina, their sole employee, has new intelligence about the Surfside Motor Inn. "Those automatic clothes dryers? They's going to have a whole room of them. Big ones, too. You can put in four, five sets of sheets at a time. Then they have these wringers, like in the big laundries up in Chicago, and they'll press the clothes just as fine as could be."

One pin, two pins, Regina hangs the sheets on the line. She clips one half, reaches for a clothes pin from her dress lapel, and then clips the other end. Sitting on the grass with Johnny, Alice wants to say to Regina, "If it's so fine on the other side of the boulevard, why don't you go work there?" But she doesn't dare because Regina just might take her up on it.

"They have those dryers and wringers in all commercial laundries," Alice says. *And if we brought our sheets there, you wouldn't have a job.*

"Yes, ma'am, they certainly do." Her "ma'am" is more of an exclamation than an act of deference.

Before they hired Regina this summer, the only black servants Alice had seen were in *Gone with the Wind*. She was not prepared for this thin, light brown woman who chain-smokes Chesterfields and corrects her constantly.

"Wish all that dust would settle. That's the trouble with hanging sheets out-of-doors."

"Mmm." Alice hates talking to Regina, but this is the only shady spot in the backyard. And she is the only one Alice has to talk to. After seeing Johnny's fat lip, and hearing the girls' breathless account of the accident, Jim has ordered her to stop driving.

"But this motor inn's going to have all that laundry equipment right there. Convenient. You just walk your sheets down to this room and in a couple of hours they be washed, dried and ironed. And I heard they's going to have the air-conditioning in every unit. So even in the summertime, those guests will be cool as a mint julep. Just press a button, and all of a sudden, it's January."

Regina makes do now with their gasoline-powered wringer washer, which Jim rigged up in the breezeway. She threads sheets in, one by one, a chore that consumes all morning. It is either that or send the linens to the Chinese laundry downtown, which isn't cheap and can take days.

"Yep, that place over there's going to be booming year around," Regina says. She pins up the last pillowcase and stands back to admire the rows of cotton flapping like sails in the wind. She pulls a pack of cigarettes from her apron pocket. "Your feet's swelling."

Alice looks at her legs, which no longer seem so long and thin.

"It's hot." Tentatively, Alice presses her left ankle. Fluid moves beneath the skin like water inside a balloon. She tries to remember her rotation on the obstetrical unit. Don't most expectant women have swollen ankles, sooner or later? Though she can't recall hers looking like this during the other pregnancies. "That's all. It's hot."

"How long they been swollen like that?" Regina speaks barely above a whisper, as though she wants no one else to hear, not Johnny, not even the unborn baby.

"I don't know." Since the accident? But it wasn't an accident, not really. "My whole body feels swollen. Standing up I can't even see my feet."

Looming over her, Regina stops inhaling, and a half-inch of ash dangles from the end of her cigarette.

"You been standing? Not supposed to be standing. That's the whole reason I'm here."

"No. Not really. I do the dishes." That very morning, before dawn, she crept out the door and over to the beach again, where she ran like a child dragging a kite. She ran and ran until she could scarcely breathe.

Regina leans down. Firmly, she places one brown hand on Alice's left ankle, then on the right. Regina's skin is not black at all but the color of leather, with fine shades of varying colors, like wood grain. She looks more like the Narragansett Indians at home than any black person Alice has seen in the movies.

"You got a mother?" Regina remains crouched but has taken her hands away and busies herself stamping out her Chesterfield in the dead grass.

"Yes, of course." Far away, beyond the horizon, too far away to see.

"Where is she?"

Alice says nothing.

"She coming down? You've got your hands full here. Woman like you, in your condition,"—and Alice knows instantly that she means *a white woman like you*— "needs her mother around."

"She's up north." When Regina continues to stare, she adds, "In Rhode Island. We grew up in Rhode Island."

"Where's that? Part of New York?"

"Nooo." She can't help a little laugh. No one in Florida seems to know any geography north of the Mason Dixon Line. "It's in New England. It's a state. South of Boston," she adds lamely.

"You might want to call her, write to her or something, tell her you need some help down here. You don't look so good, if you don't mind me saying so."

Alice's eyes fill. Is it the truth of the statement that upsets her, or the fact that this near stranger has noticed something her husband refuses to acknowledge? Of course, she doesn't look good. Though she avoids mirrors, even the small one on the medicine chest, she imagines what they would reflect: ashy pallor, under-eye circles, bloated skin. But as long as no one mentions it, she can stumble along, knowing each evening brings her another day closer to the end of this pregnancy, and the sickness it has brought. When this baby is finally out, she will ask – no, demand – that the doctor tie her tubes. That will mean, of course, going to Halifax Hospital instead of Palm, which is owned by the Catholic Church.

"I've had seven babies," Regina says. "My sister's had five, and I've got a sister-in-law who's a midwife. I used to clean the maternity ward over at Palm Hospital. When a woman starts to swell up like you—"

Alice can't let her go on. "I'm fine. It's just this blasted heat."

197

Regina stands. She picks up a few stray clothes pins and tosses them into the wicker basket. She turns as though to say something else, but then she passes Alice and heads back to the motel. Her calves are muscular, her ankle bones sharp, as though she has spent a lifetime walking in the sand dunes, not on a Florida beach as flat as pavement.

Alice cannot write to Mother again. She hasn't replied to her last letter, more than a week ago. And what would she say? *I am unwell.* The last news Marjorie needs to hear. Of the three, Alice is the one their mother worries about the least, and that is how Alice prefers it. *We have something in common, Mother and I,* she thinks; *we like to mother other people but don't particularly want to be mothered ourselves.*

She cannot confide in Lenore. Her letters are short and strained, their tone melancholy. When Alice writes back – sometimes weeks later – she tries to be cheerful, encouraging. *The baby will grow out of colic,* she assures her, and *What a good teacher you must be – we are all so proud.* Alice can't tell her that motherhood doesn't get easier, that exhaustion is a permanent condition, that she would be crazy to go back to the school. If Alice ever confided in her how she felt about this pregnancy, it would only confirm Lenore's worst fears.

It is Meredith that Alice longs to talk to. But by now their middle sister has ascended a mountain high in the Smokies, where even a carrier pigeon couldn't find her. She has the freedom that both Lenore and Alice long for, that Mother seized with both hands as soon as Daddy's funeral ended. Meredith has no one to keep her warm at night, true; but she isn't at the mercy of her body the way Lenore and Alice are. She doesn't have a husband dragging her far from home, or babies to tend, or swollen ankles and an aching back. But even though she's never been married or carried a child, Alice knows she could trust Meredith with a secret. She would not judge. She would not overreact. She would know just what to do.

The next morning, before light, Alice sneaks out of the bedroom, through the kitchen and out the office door. On bare feet she runs across the wide and empty Route 1, over the oil-stained concrete apron of the Texaco station, down the vacant alleyway next to the new hotel. At this hour even the carpenters have yet to start work. On the roof of the Surfside Motor Inn, flaps of tar paper snap, and a breeze whines an eerie song through the empty dormers. At last, her feet touch sand.

She walks all the way to her favorite piling and leans against it. The beach, too, is deserted. She might as well be the only soul alive. Her eyes sweep north along the shoreline and then over the sea. Out there, under a pale rose sky, flows a deep blue ribbon. The Gulf Stream. She watches its relentless pull northward. Those waters are bound for Cape Cod, where their warmth will finally dissolve. For some creatures, who cannot adapt to the North Atlantic, this will mark the end of their range. It is only the beginning of Alice's. She is not meant for this torrid place, where you can enjoy the beach only at dawn, where the relentless heat is unbearable half the year. Her habitat is the dunes of the Rhode Island shore. Watch Hill, Misquamicut, Weekapaug. Somehow, before this baby comes, she must find her way home.

Resolved, she pushes off the piling and turns to go. Just then, in the distance, she sees a lone figure emerge from the new motel's shadows.

It is Jim.

* * *

Since the episode on the beach, Jim and Alice have barely spoken. She has never seen him so furious. Again, she hung her head and took it. He was right, of course. She has no right to run off by herself. Even at dawn when the family still slept. As if that wasn't bad enough, she nearly smashed up the car, with all three children aboard. Doesn't she realize how dangerous her behavior is?

Of course, she does. No matter how homesick she feels, she must focus on her family. She has two daughters and a baby to tend, and another on the way. A motel to run, and a husband who needs her.

This morning he seems to have thawed. He makes the girls lunch and gives them a ride to camp. He brings a chair to the front office so Alice no longer has to perch on that ridiculous stool. He squeezes her shoulder as she sits down. He then brings Johnny out to lie on the carpet so Alice can keep an eye on him.

Jim has just walked out to the pool site when the phone rings.

"I'm worried about your sister," Mother says. She must mean Lenore. "She didn't sound right last night."

Outside a panel van pulls up. A man in a white uniform gets

199

out and opens its back double doors. The vehicle has been so hastily converted that a red cross is still visible under its white paint.

"Maybe she was tired," Alice says. From the back the driver lifts a large spray of carnations, lilies and glads. All Alice can see behind the spiky blooms is the white bill of his cap.

"You would think he'd take her out for her anniversary, instead she was cooking all day, and you can imagine how that went."

"Their anniversary." Alice forgot. She should have sent a card, at least.

"She made a gelatin mold and put *pineapple* in it."

"Just a minute, Mother, someone's here." Alice puts her hand over the mouthpiece. Before she can stop the man, he sets the flowers on the counter. "There must be some mistake. The funeral home is two streets down, on the right."

"No mistake." He holds out the card, on which has been typed Pink Azalea Motor Court, 1506 Ridgewood Ave., Daytona Beach.

"Alice? For heaven's sake, this is costing me a fortune."

"Flowers for somebody. I'm sorry, Mother, what were you saying?" With effort Alice gets up, opens the cash register, and passes the man a quarter.

"I think they're in trouble, is what I think."

"Trouble?" Sitting back down, Alice cradles the receiver against her neck and rips open the card. It reads, *My dear Alice. To the best wife a man could ask for. Love, Jim.*

"Yes, trouble. If he's not coming home from the mill, you know where he is."

"Has Lenore said anything about it?" Alice stares at the card. His words on the beach still ring in her ears: *Get back into the office where you belong.*

"You know Lenore. She wouldn't say anything. She's determined to make this marriage work. She was bull-headed enough to marry him. I knew this would come to a bad end. And that baby! Oh, poor Henry."

Alice has yet to meet her new nephew. Mother said he is colicky and underweight. She blames Lenore for refusing to bottle-feed him. But maybe Lenore is onto something; maybe Alice

200

herself should be nursing her baby.

"Why don't you talk to her? Pay her a visit. I'm sure she could use some help."

"I don't want to get roped into babysitting. You should hear him howl after he's been fed. I've never heard anything like it."

"He's colicky." Alice sighs. "Just go over there, you know, talk to her, like you'd talk to me."

"Oh, Alice, for heaven's sake, there is no comparison." This time Mother sighs. Alice hears her swallow, and imagines her glass of iced tea, a sprig of mint floating in it. "You know how she is. She never tells you what she's really feeling."

"I can't afford to call her, or I would," Alice says finally. "But I will write to her. I owe her a letter." Truth be told, Alice owes her more than one. She can never quite figure out what to say to Lenore.

"All right." Alice senses her mother's goodbye before she says it. She can see her standing up, looking out the picture window of her new house, smoothing out the pleats of her dress. She has roses to clip, or a library book to return. Suddenly Alice misses her terribly.

"And Mother," she starts to say, but Marjorie has hung up.

Jim stands by the road next to the motel sign, where a pale blue Cadillac has pulled up. Its driver puts a large, square briefcase on the ground and fans a handful of colorful pictures.

"The hand-tinted linen is still quite fine, but some people prefer the black-and-white photograph. I've sold two lines of them this week."

Jim, absorbed in the samples, does not notice Alice's approach.

"Of course, you have a colorful place here. Azaleas and all." The salesman looks up and smiles at her. "How do, ma'am."

"Hello, honey." Jim smiles quickly and turns back to the man. "What about the pool? Can't we wait until it's done?"

"We can airbrush that right out of the negative. All of our hand-tinted lines are color-corrected. We'll just put some grass there, for now."

"But I want the pool to be on the postcard," Jim says.

"That's the whole point."

"We can paint it in, then. Fill in the hole with blue water."

Shifting her weight from the left leg to the right, and back again, Alice feels the baby tumble lazily. Her scalp prickles with heat. She has a straw hat, but Jim doesn't like people seeing her in it. He says it makes her look like a Cracker.

"All right," Jim says. He shakes the man's hand.

"There's just the matter of lettering."

Why they are conversing out here, in the sun, instead of in the fan-cooled office, Alice has no idea. But maybe Jim doesn't want her around – doesn't want to complicate the transaction with a pregnant wife who frets about the looming hospital bill. Not to mention the flowers. What did they cost?

"The Chamber gives us a set of postcards every year," she reminds him.

"Honey, why don't you go inside? You really need to stay off your feet."

"Everyone has them, ma'am," the salesman says. Remarkably, he does not seem to be sweating. His gray linen suit and white boater are spotless; his shoes, white and brown wingtips, look freshly polished. "Why, the new hotel across the street just ordered five hundred, and they're not even open yet."

He probably already used that line on Jim. "But we only have a dozen units."

"Multiply it out," he says. "Dozen times three-hundred and sixty-five days, that's more than four thousand cards a year."

"We're not booked all year," she insists. "This is our slow season -"

"You will be once people start sending these cards. Postcards get results. People like to show off to the folks back home. 'Having a wonderful time,' and all that. It's advertising, you understand."

Jim's jaw has begun to set. Whatever softening the flowers indicated disappears as he looks from Alice to the salesman and back again. "Let me handle this, Alice. You really need to get out of the heat."

"I have some typography samples," the man says. "After that, I can write up your order, and then I'll take the photographs."

"How much is all this going to cost?" Maybe it is the way the salesman turned back to Jim, or her husband's none-too-subtle attempt to get rid of her. Whatever the reason, Alice plants her swollen feet firmly in the grass, unwilling and unable to turn and leave the men to their business.

"Quite reasonable," the man says. "Minimum one-hundred count, one image only. Discount for veterans."

"Where's the baby?" Jim interrupts.

"He's napping." She put Johnny in his crib and came out to thank Jim for the flowers. Now here she is, skirting her duties again, failing to be a good wife.

"Hadn't you better check on him?"

"Discount for veterans," the salesman repeats, a little louder. "What branch of service?"

Alice smiles sweetly at the salesman. "Why don't you come into our office? It's cooler inside. I can get you a Coca-Cola."

"You go check on the baby," Jim repeats. "We'll be along presently."

"Army Air Force myself. European Theater. Almost ended up in the Pacific, but they dropped the bombs, thank God."
Jim doesn't say anything. For a moment they stand there. The baby has stopped kicking but seems to be moving, pressing downward, almost as if she is in labor.

"Go along," Jim says, teeth gritted. "We'll be there in a minute."

"Let me guess. You look like a tough guy to me. Marine? Guadalcanal, Iwo Jima?"

Her back seizes up and she lets out an involuntary "Oh." She should go back to the office but somehow, she cannot. She should cover for her husband. She should have some compassion for him, having to face these questions all the time, no matter how far away they run. But instead, she waits to see what he would say.

"Honey, we really don't want Johnny waking up alone again," Jim says. His hands clench and unclench. She tries to picture the right hand with a pen in it, writing out that card, but she cannot.

"Ten percent. Just need to see your honorable discharge. Keep it official, you understand."

Inside her, something lets go. For a moment she thinks her water has broken, but what trickles down her legs is red. Down her thighs, over her knobby knees, to her biscuit-sized ankles.

She feels, rather than hears, the salesman's sharp intake of breath. Then the wind, too, seems to inhale and exhale, shaking the palm trees and stirring up a dust devil in the hole of Jim's pool. Clods of dirt hit her legs.

"Alice! For God's sake, get in the house." Jim's voice is strangled, as though someone holds him by the throat.

She waddles slowly back across the pavement. A clump of red splatters to the ground. She has no idea what is happening. False labor? Or is she losing the baby? But Jim seems to care about nothing but his own disgust. Before she reaches the office steps, she yells back, "Thanks for the flowers." But her words disappear into the swaying palms.

The doctor does not seem concerned, but puts Alice on bed rest anyway. "Nothing amiss, Mrs.," he says with a chuckle. He calls all of his patients "Mrs.," so he doesn't have to remember their names, Alice supposes. "Baby is just feeling his oats. A little placenta discharged. Nothing to be alarmed over. But just in case, stay in bed for a week. Get those pretty daughters of yours to help out."

They sit in the waiting room, Darcy and Ellen, swinging their legs in unison. Johnny fusses in Darcy's lap. She lugged him into the building so Alice didn't have to. A tiny spark of sadness flickers in her seven-year-old's eyes. She is too young to be worried about her mother.

"Don't worry," Alice tells them. "Mommy just needs to go to bed for a while."

The girls do not complain. They volunteer to make their own lunches. But when Alice breaks the news to Jim, he takes it as some grim punishment aimed at making his life miserable. He tucks her into bed, but then recites all the ways she has brought this on herself.

"Alice, you have to be careful. Keep out of the heat. Stay off your feet. You have to be responsible."

She nods.

"And that car accident. You could have lost the baby."

"There was no accident." She tries to say more, but he keeps going.

"You hit the steering wheel. That strikes me as an accident."

"I just stopped short, was all." She waves her hand vaguely. "The girls were talking, that's all, I looked back at them for a second."

"And you've been sitting outside on that damp ground, talking to Regina," he goes on. "I gave you a perfectly good chair in the office."

"Yes. And I appreciate it." She turns her head to the pillow and closes her eyes. There will be no more morning escapes to the beach. She will not run on the sand or lean against her piling. She will no longer lie outdoors in the shade. From now on, she will stay in bed, trying as hard as she can to be the wife he expects.

* * *

Alice dreams of motorcycles. They start at one end of Daytona Beach, skid on corners of sand, race onto the road and then circle back to the beach, leaving trails like snakeskin. Their roar obliterates everything – the surf, the gulls' cries, the hum of a blimp overhead. Here she knows no one and no one knows her. She stands anonymously in the throng of cheering onlookers, neither pumping her fists nor cheering nor jeering. She wants to get to the water. She tries to cross the motorcycles' path, or rather make it across the sand before the clumps of riders return, but each time she starts out, she hears engines growling, and the lead machine cuts her off. "I'm going to have a baby," she says to the man next to her. "I need to be in the water." He looks down at her and laughs. "You ain't having no baby," he says. "And if you are, you've got a pool, don't you?"

She wakes to the clatter of the fan. The sun blasts through the drawn bedroom curtain. Of course, there are no motorcycles on Daytona now; the riders will not return until February, when the motel will be booked solid for a week. The races resumed this winter after a hiatus for the war. So many tourists showed up that people in town had to open up their homes. Jim jacked up the price of the cabins, until someone reported him to the Chamber of

Commerce. Though it was a profitable winter, she hated all of it: the grease of the engines; the tracks cutting up the beach; the grandstands that took over the dunes.

She does not want to be here for another Daytona 200, but the dream was not about motorcycles. Why did she try to get to the ocean? Why did the man say she wasn't going to have a baby? A chill ripples over her stomach and around to her back. She rises on her elbows. Johnny peers through the slats of his crib. His tongue works in his mouth, slipping out quickly like a lizard's and then back again. He cannot have been awake long or he would be fussing.

Although the doctor has lifted the bed-rest order, Alice is not supposed to pick up the baby. She does so anyway. His skin sticks to hers, and he keeps bobbing his head against her shoulder bones, hard, until she has to hold him back with one hand. One baby could be so unlike his siblings. Or perhaps she is not the same mother she was with Darcy and Ellen—older, now, with less energy, and too soon pregnant again. She has not enjoyed one full day with him, nor he with her, so they both have been robbed. She thinks of Lenore suddenly, and Mother, and wonders if whatever has gone wrong between them has similar roots. The thought disturbs her even more than the dream man's dark prophecy.

Before he can butt her shoulder again, she kisses the top of Johnny's head. Maybe it isn't too late.

In the afternoon Jim pronounces the pool completed. A truck will arrive any minute to fill it, and he wants them all to go outside and watch. The girls, who have just returned from a day of swimming at the Y, are still in their suits but do not look enthusiastic. Johnny has finally gone down for a nap, and even though Jim perversely wants his witness, too, Alice refuses to disturb him. The thermometer in the shade of the breezeway reads 92 degrees.

The water tanker drives onto their last strip of grass, taking out a pink azalea. A burly man in blue work pants and a coffee-colored shirt hops out of the cab and begins unspooling a hose. She assumed they would just use the garden hose to fill the pool, but Jim laughed at that suggestion. "It would take forever, and drain the well in the process," he said. Now water begins pouring from the truck to the pool. It sounds like a waterfall, or the surf off Daytona. Occasionally the hose bucks or skips, like a snake, but as the water level rises, these motions slow until the hose falls still, as though satiated in some way.

"Whoa," Jim calls to the driver, motioning with his left hand. With enormous effort, the driver pulls back on the wheel that controls the water's flow until it ceases altogether. Water sloshes and slaps over the sides of the pool until it, too, rocks gently and then stops. The man operates a winch that recoils the hose, and the engine drowns out everything—the traffic on Route 1, the distant surf, and the conversation between Jim and the man. There are waves and handshakes, cash exchanged and good feeling all around until the driver climbs into the cab and slowly rolls the tanker back over the ruined lawn, taking out another azalea as he leaves.

"A-ho." Jim waves to her. He looks happier than she has seen him in ages. He has birthed his pool, while she still waddles about, like a child hefting a watermelon.

"Well." She tries to smile. The pool is impressive: he has lined it with delft tiles, and the water shines aquamarine in the sun.

He leans down and reaches into a corner. "Filter," he says. "And heater. Won't need the heater this time of year, of course."

"It's wonderful, Jim." Her lungs have started to close. She is in no shape to replant the azaleas, but someone will have to do it.

"Eventually, we'll get a diving board," he says. "Right here, on the deep end. And a canopy. So mothers can relax while their kids go swimming."

"Well," she says again. "It will increase the value of the place, won't it?"

He frowns. "I suppose. The point is we'll be booked solid all year round. We'll be able to compete with those new hotels on the beach."

He will never sell this place. They will never go home. This pool is a part of him as surely as the sand of Watch Hill is a part of her. She should have realized much sooner what it meant, and what it would lead to: more improvements, more investments, grander schemes. All of it weighing her down in Florida like an anchor.

Darcy and Ellen, recovered from camp, wander over. "Can we go for a dip? Can we, Dad?" Ellen asks.

He hesitates. "All right. But rinse your feet first. And remember, you can never go in the pool unless one of us is here."

The girls hose off their feet, run to the shallow end and lower themselves into the water. Darcy kicks off and heads toward them in quick, even strokes. Ellen, not far behind her, clearly struggles with technique but keeps herself buoyant. Alice longs to join them. But despite growing up by the ocean, she never learned to swim. None of them did.

"I've been thinking," Jim says. "It might be time to buy some more land. That lot behind us could be drained. We could add some units."

With effort she lowers herself to a sitting position on the pool's edge and dips in her feet. Pieces of grass float up.

"I think I could get it for a good price, maybe twenty-five, twenty-seven hundred. We could add another dozen cabins, or build out a motel. Or even—what do you think about this – add a diner on the end."

Darcy continues to do laps, slipping through the water like an otter, but Ellen's strokes have flagged. She hangs onto the pool's edge, wiping her mouth. "She should come out," Alice says, without looking up at him. "They both should."

"You don't seem very excited."

She is about to snap something back at him—for how can she get excited about the prospect of more rooms to clean and a diner to run, while taking care of four children?—when Ellen's head slips under. One second, she is yelling for Darcy, and the next, she is gone, leaving only a small ripple of water behind her.

Frozen, Alice tries to scream. She grabs hold of Jim's leg and finally the words come out. As soon as he realizes what is happening, he dives in. But Darcy gets there before he does. Alice sees her disappear too, diving straight down like a dolphin, and then surface with her limp sister. When Jim reaches them, Ellen lies prone on the concrete on the other side of the pool, coughing up water. By the time Alice makes it over there, Ellen has begun to cry. Darcy places her two small hands over her sister's back and keeps her face down, pumping at her lungs to expel the water. Somehow, although Ellen's swimming skills remain weak, Darcy has learned not just to swim, but to save someone who cannot.

Ellen has not swallowed much water after all. She was under for seconds. But Jim runs for a blanket, and they wrap her up carefully before carrying her to the car. Darcy and Alice watch him spin out of the driveway and skid over the ruts left by the pool tanker. Then they go inside to wake the baby.

* * *

Jim returns hours later. Ellen, still in a damp swimsuit, looks as though she's been threaded through the wringer washer. Without a word Alice takes her from Jim and leads her into the bathroom, where she peels off her daughter's swimsuit and runs a hot bath. Ellen screams and kicks. "I don't want to go in! I don't want to!" she keeps saying, but finally Alice convinces her. As soon as she feels the water, Ellen's eyes grow heavy. With difficulty, Alice bends over the tub and washes her gently – the knobby knees, the long arms, the mottled skin on her back where Darcy pushed and pressed. Then she wraps Ellen in a towel and hugs her and noses her face into the crook between the girl's neck and shoulder, inhaling her smell, mixed with chlorine and some hospital odor, perhaps antiseptic.

"My baby," she says over and over. "My sweet baby." Ellen hiccups and Alice forces herself to stop. There is no use in showing the girl how frightened she was.

The doctors said she will be fine, she didn't inhale much water, most of it ending up in her stomach. But they are to watch her carefully over the next few days. If she develops a cough or a temperature, they must bring her to the hospital immediately.

Jim tells Alice all this after she puts Ellen to bed. He sits at the kitchen table, having a cup of coffee. None of them have eaten dinner. Alice gave Darcy bread and butter before bed, but Ellen's throat is sore and she still feels nauseous.

"You have to drain it." Alice refuses to sit down, instead gripping the back of a kitchen chair.

"What are you talking about?"

"The pool. Drain it. I can't spend every moment worrying about them. If Johnny fell in, I couldn't save him."

"There is no 'drain.' This isn't the kitchen sink, Alice. It's an

209

in-ground pool. At the end of the season, the tanker will come back and reverse the process. But that costs money."

"I don't care what it costs. I'll call them myself."

"You will do no such thing," he hisses. He looks toward the girls' bedroom and lowers his voice, but now it contains more menace. "I just broke my back, not to mention our bank account, building the finest swimming pool along this stretch. It will make us significant money this winter, and it might even increase our bookings now. We are not going to abandon it because Ellen had a little accident."

"A little accident?" He speaks as if she skinned her knee or bumped her head on the carport. "She was unconscious. She almost drowned."

"That's all the more reason to keep her at the Y. Look at Darcy. What a champ she was today. She never lost her cool. Of course, I could have done the same—"

Alice inhales loudly, holds her breath for a second longer than necessary, and exhales. "We cannot count on our seven-year-old girl to be a lifeguard."

"I didn't say that. But swimming is a life skill. Instead of asking me to drain the pool, you should sign up for swimming lessons. And as soon as Johnny can walk, take him with you."

For a moment she sees herself at the YMCA, in a tent-like bathing suit, gradually lowering her body into the water. She would sink to the bottom just as Ellen did, baby and all. Pregnant or not, she will never float, not at the Y pool, not in their pool, not in the salty Atlantic Ocean.

Already she is up to her neck, and soon the water will push her under for good.

* * *

First Alice packs a small bag, the smallest in their set of luggage. The size of the suitcase belies her intentions. She folds her favorite pink maternity dress, the one with sprigs of flowers on the hem, the good dress she has been saving to come home from the hospital in. She adds a nightgown, another dress, two changes of underwear and some toiletries. Carefully she slides her velvet pouch under the luggage's ripped lining, then leaves the suitcase in an obvious place, at the foot of their bed, just the spot an expectant mother would

210

put her overnight bag.

The other suitcase presents more difficulty. She could pack it when Jim is out of the apartment, but she cannot leave it in the open; it must immediately be locked into the Packard's trunk. Lifting it presents another problem. She could enlist Regina's help, but she doesn't need to be Alice's co-conspirator, and besides, Alice does not entirely trust the maid. Of the girls, Darcy is the one least likely to tattle to her father, but again, it seems unfair to require such an adult deception from a girl who already has shouldered more than her share of the load.

On her surreptitious trips to the beach, Alice imagined what it would be like to fly home, like a seagull, or float on the Gulf Stream, buffeted by a pod of whales or manatees. Since that fanciful daydream has taken on the hard edge of necessity, the only way out of Florida is Route 1 north. Through Georgia and the Carolinas, Virginia and Maryland, Delaware and New Jersey. On the maps from the Packard's glove compartment her finger follows the road, a black line snaking north that disappears in a maze of spider webs just outside New York City. She can manage it. She will have to.

For the dream of motorcycles and the ocean was an omen. She must not leave her babies here in this hothouse, with the pool beckoning its evil watery eye and Jim planning ever more elaborate traps to keep them here. It is time to go home.

IN THE OCEAN OF
LOST BELONGINGS

RONDA PISZK BROATCH

I sometimes feel beautiful. Sometimes
I comb the beach, looking for the scrim
of denial, but it burrows into packed sand
wet with clams and geoducks. Truth be told,

I am an owl on a summer day, open
window, an eyeless mask in gilt. Guilty
here and now, fixed between signposts past
and future, my pockets full of God stitched

with hummingbird precision. Sometimes I lose
sleep. Does she have her rain boots? Does he
have enough sugar to sweeten his blood?
I sometimes doze when the ship goes down.

The day I washed up in an ocean of loss
it was my mind I missed the most.

TEA PARTY IN THE
SOUTHERN SEA

CHRISTIANA JASUTAN

I wear green and let the ocean munch me with its teeth,
head-first like going for a kiss. Around the salt I see
life unfold like oxygen, each fin laced with air
bubbles, each clam opens and closes like hungry mouths.

The princess asks if I bring an open heart into her palms,
I ask if that's always the first thing she says. I ask if she's lonely
with hollow-eyed men marching with her name on their tongues,
brimming with adoration that spills to their jaw

like bubbling spit. I wonder when love starts feeling like
unending waves; ebbing and flowing and giving nothing
but braids on sand. I wonder if love will be light
as seafoam, saltwater on your lips.

Nyai*, I bring tea with me because that is the only way I keep warm
on some days. Perhaps the ocean is unforgiving, perhaps your kingdom
is a ceaseless cold. But you can't see the tears underwater.

She smiles and says: *the Southern Sea is with you.*

*Nyai Roro Kidul, Indonesian Goddess of the sea (Queen of the Southern Sea
in Sundanese and Javanese mythology)*

THE SYLVIA PLATH
OF ANYTHING

ABIGAIL ECKSTINE

I don't need to tell my dreams to everyone
Somedays it just feels like the end of the world—
Twined topsy-turvy thoughts,
Follow me to the installation of the dark vacuum,
The way of the world is one thing
Bites of blood pudding between dinner
Solitude is like being four and licking the window
Or shooting stars back into the sky,

Men are meat
Woman daily bread
Cats the water that sustain me
Find me sheep
To bring back into the fold,

To lie between the rocks at sea
Before death would be heaven
To let the tide carry me out to sea
I was born to die and find everything in between

CORPUS FEMINA

ZOË MORGAN

Here is the corpus of a woman in bloom
Entangled by the red ribbons of octopus limbs,
tongued tentacles
Drip sticky gloop on
Pale
Venus-virgin   petals.

While only her foetus is safe under water
In the firm cellophane
Of a lonesome jellyfish;
Aglow,
on a
Spongey
[but tepid]   bed.

She's naked & oh
Creature's audacity:
A starfish tickled her nose
And divided her flesh!
Quickening
she succumbed, sneezed, and bled   that saccharine death.

[A thousand petals wafting
loose and lost in a floral saliva sea.]

What is sublime?
These petals are beautiful
Warm-blooded red as our lady's breast
Smeared on the legs of sea-beasts

Not all gloom
By some good fortune we later found remnants of shells
Accumulated secretions particles
Pollen.
They washed up on the shore years later, whispering:
"Fists are budding flowers in bloom and
Our woman is made of sand"

You can walk along the coast now and probably see
A huge footprint of
Ribboned petals aglow or
A handcuffed tentacle leg
Swept up in *ink* and sea foam.

COLD DAUGHTER

KIRI DELANDÉ

My mother wished for a cold daughter / girl with icicle teeth / blizzard blustering through my body / a subtle violence so quiet as I kiss you goodnight / I was hypothermia with swinging hips / a fucked-up frostbitten fairy / unsanctimonious unseelie / drinking blood like aged fine wine

She fed me marbled seal meat / had me suckle on the tusks of walruses / I wrestled with wolves and limped away the loser / as blood wept through / my midnight-kissed skin / she packed snow and salt on my wounds / sneered / *get colder*

Many winter nights spent / with hail glittering down my cheeks / my icicle bones breaking / under her monstrous might / I think my mother was a cold daughter / Shiva shuddered / as she slipped from her womb / and said to face her / with a glacial heart

An avalanche ascends in my abdomen / as I erupt from my ancestral home / Mother / you never supped with a sumptuous flame / never coveted a candle's wick / your roaring violence ignited as I kiss you goodbye / but just once I would love to feel it / just once / just once / just once

THE WEDDING GUEST

MARIA O'BRIEN

White flesh swells before me, rippled like the wild tides it had been snatched from. As though the pressure of the environment in which it was formed marked it eternally with its own distinct print.

I arch my wrist and stab.

Perched on the top of my fork, the plump, clean muscle glistens with a smear of garlic butter. The chance gathering of garnish at the center brings to mind an occupation with eyes, which pervaded much of my youth. Unlike most children, I inherited an ocularist's toolkit from my late grandfather.

Strange to be suddenly thrown back to one's school days while eating butterfly lobster and a mixed bean salad in a hotel room at forty-three years of age. But weddings have that peculiar effect of amplifying the passage of time. Especially when it is a childhood friend in the position of groom. Poor David lost an eye in a tussle with a rabid dog at six years of age and came to me, the quiet girl with the glass eye collection, in hope of a miracle. That's how we became friends. I can still see his pale pudding cheeks propping up a Mickey Mouse eyepatch as he perused the hazel, ebony, sable irises in tentative search for his match.

I couldn't give him an eye, of course, but I did give him what an avid collector of strange and mysterious objects can give anyone—an insatiable obsession, a lifelong distraction. However, his eye collection was different to mine. His eyes were very much alive and required effort and precision to be caught, as so many little boys prefer their triumphs to be. Eyes in this case being the illusionary artwork of the butterfly—he was an amateur lepidopterist.

I pop the white bulge in my mouth. With a satisfied sigh, my shoulders release, filling the soft fluffy bathrobe in which I have cocooned myself. The television plays in front of the bed on mute. A picture of a stone building fills the screen. This time when I fork another mouthful, taste vacates my sensory faculties. My neural pathways struggle to patch together the fragments of information needed to comprehend this surreal vision before me.

As the images flash on the television, I note the Palladian entrance, the purple sea of coneflowers rippling out from the front windows, the weeping willow stationed to the far right of the building, the gravel carpark with my red Peugeot peeking out from behind a single-decker coach. There is no doubt the report is of the very hotel I am sitting in right now.

My mouth freezes, leaving the pureed fish to stew in a pool of salivary juices. Breaking news bulletins glide across the bottom of the screen: *Homicide at the Admiral Manor Hotel.*

A double rap sounds from the door. Despite my brimming tears and the vengeful lobster rising in my stomach, I swallow hard, and go to answer.

* * *

Yesterday had been a spectacular wedding, the April date chosen for the cherry blossoms being in full bloom, transforming the outdoor ceremony into a whimsical froth of sky. My assigned dinner companions at the reception delighted in their knowledge that the eight mature trees had been specially transported across the country for the big day, all in honor of the bride's name, Sakura, which is Japanese for cherry blossom. She is indeed worthy of the name, being a beautiful thing in herself: big emotive eyes, elegant limbs, a model in fact. I expected nothing less for David's bride.

A college friend of his regaled me with how the pair met. Sakura had been framed in white, her long black hair billowing in the air blower positioned at her right foot; one of his models both then and now. She is big in Japan, "as the song goes," the friend quipped with practiced timing, but not so much here. David brought her home to America. He saw her potential and knew just how to harness it – by stringing her up in a big glass box above Bryant Square. He had grown bored of still pictures, dead things; his art was coming to life. Of course, she said yes, and all they had left to do was pin down a wedding date.

Finding myself at his wedding was a source of amusement. A small revelation came in receiving that embossed linen invitation in my letterbox. It must've been twenty-five years since I last saw David. The internationally famous photographer remembers me after all!

As I navigated the hotel to the ceremony that morning, I could've been walking through walls like a haunting ghost. A silly thought perhaps, but one never does know the true purpose of a wedding invite: to bump up numbers? To rub one's nose in their smug success? A pity invite? Or worse, one of guilt.

But I didn't truly believe my heralding was for any one of these reasons. In fact, in my daydreaming throughout the nuptials, watching Sakura's eyelashes flutter behind the tails of her veil, I concluded that I was there for the same reason the lobster wears its shell, the butterfly its wings, and David his pearlescent marble lodged into his socket. I always have been.

I've read that our very first memory of any heightened experience remains intact in our minds forever, acting as bookmarks throughout our lifetime, hallmarks of our identity. I would imagine the first wrapping of one's fingers around a neck would qualify as noteworthy.

I still remember, even now.

* * *

David's mother, being neurotic and Irish, had kept the main room at the front of their home in a perpetual state of suspended animation. It was as though the room had been swept up in one giant gulp of breath, never to be released. Despite a somber oak dining table making up ninety percent of its contents, the space seemed to collect shadows. Darkness caught in the floral net curtain, sliding out from underneath the chair legs, creating black bars across the paisley carpet when the sun peeped in from the west. In that dusky half-light, the room assumed an abandoned gloom. Sanitized and forbidden except for study, we would play in it any chance we could. It was where he first showed me his collection.

At that young age, I believed the very purpose of that room was to house the butterflies.

"Pinning is an art form," he told me. He kept his collection in a drawer of the large wooden cabinet. Hidden from the light of day, each butterfly's mystique lay dormant until a child's hand arrived with a soft pull of a handle.

I can still hear the creak of the rail as he drew out their resting carcasses, each one impaled through the thorax with a stainless-steel pin. They had died from suffocation in a glass killing jar. He pointed out the midnight blue of the Red-Spotted Purple and the lemon yellow of the Cloudless Sulphur, each of them tantalizingly vivid.

Alone in the room after David's mother called for him, I felt like a convict being handed the keys to my cell. Lifting off the glass case was easy.

* * *

After dessert, silverware disappeared back into the kitchen, and everyone was graced with a flute of champagne to watch the bride and groom dance a waltz.

Between the ceremony and the reception, Sakura transformed from an ivory figurine to a shimmering angel in a ballgown of rolling silk-chiffon. With her tresses and pink swathes swinging in time, she floated around the dancefloor with David's left hand pinned to the center of her back. The smooth line of her jaw struck forward towards her audience.

Again, I pictured her in the magazine spread of the Bryant Square photoshoot. David had dressed her in oversized petals and immobilized her within the glass box inscribed with *The rose that lives its little hour Is prized beyond the sculpted flower.* The journalist covering the piece really did slaver over that clever detail. The exhibition announced David's artistic transformation to the world.

All at once, the music gained an extra beat and the room merged at the middle with brothers and sisters, aunts and uncles, old friends and new entangled in their simultaneous expression of approval and joy. I finished off my glass from my place at the table, watching the past and future collide like a car crash behind my eyes.

* * *

"You can't get it right the first time," young David told me. He toyed with the killing jar in his hands. "You have to practice on lesser butterflies and moths first before you try to pin the beautiful ones."

I gazed down at his limited collection of prized specimens and wondered how many of their kind had been sacrificed on account of

221

aesthetic mediocrity. Following the arc of the outer margin of a wing, down to the kiss where the two flaps meet, I could see my freckled forehead in the reflection of the glass, my drooping eyes, my thin lips. My finger just grazed the velvet fur of a wing when David caught me by the throat. In his eye, I watched the revelation unfold, from impassioned anger to fear and then to something else.

* * *

Outside it was night, not that any of the wedding guests would care to know. The room curled in on itself, shoulders starting to slump, couples draping across each other, children coiling up tight as foxes under tables. I crossed the room to the bar and ordered myself a nightcap. With my snifter in hand, I approached the ice sculpture, which mere hours ago had been a buxom rose. Now it appeared hacked to death by a particularly malicious lawnmower. I grasped the ice pick and chipped a chunk off into my glass.

From where I stood, I had the view of an opening into an adjoining room where David walked through, seeming to follow the glow of the midnight moon and, like a somnambulist rising from my bed, I followed.

I found him smoking a cigar within a glass conservatory protruding from the back of the hotel. It seemed an honest mistake to me that I had walked off with the ice pick instead of my whiskey glass. But I could not deny the symbolism presented to me as I stood in the doorway. In that moment, he could've been a moth spiraling around a porch light and I, a child with visions of violence in my heart.

A MEMORY OF TOUCH

LIZZIE WANN

my silver hair falls in waves
like whitecaps on a restless sea

once I fanned it all above me
she ran her fingers through it

blissful sensation
disarming intimacy

she was not my lover
but there was safety with her

satisfaction of a stubborn door
clicking as it catches the latch

LILIANA

SERENA PICCOLI

I am the grandmother of that little girl
who was expelled at the age of 8 from school
we're Jews—Dad said.

I have a name now and am still Jewish

I am the grandmother of that little girl
hairless skeleton in Auschwitz
no color\time\senses

The dog was watching, the guard was beating up bones
some bread in the excrement was her lunch
the girl with no breasts\age\period\underpants

I have a name now, my identity

The girl was digging holes for water pipes
every hour every day
but no time existed, only bones, smoke, and ashes

When she picked up a dried apricot out of the camp
she tasted freedom again
and started repeating
memory keeps democracy healthy

I am the grandmother of that little girl who gives me no peace
because it is war—always
because fascism never died and can kill in the most innocent guise

I am the mother of all of you who keep fighting
and will fight
the abomination that I've survived

I am Liliana, still with that number on my arm
I will die as I have lived
with history on my skin

This poem is dedicated to Liliana Segre, an Italian Holocaust survivor, named Senator for life by Italian President Sergio Mattarella in 2018 for outstanding patriotic merits in the social field.

ODE TO OLYMPE DE GOUGES

WENDY BOOYDEGRAAFF

You were born someone else, in a world ruled by men.
You didn't stop asking *Why?* Why were men legislating,
voting, autocratically deciding fates? Why, indeed.

You chose a name worthy of your fight, reinvented, defended
rights of women—all people, all humans—spoke against slavery.
For if one of us is in bondage, is not the whole system in bondage?

And if the system is in bondage, are we not, the people of the system,
also in bondage? Every one of us? You kept company with radicals,
thought and fought for equality. Still rings radical today when women

make less than men, when Black and Native peoples are killed at
higher numbers by the very people that are under oath to keep order,
when some don't eat while others leave full plates at multiple palatial
estates. 1789, 1791,

2021, still fighting the same fight. *Les Droits de la Femme et de la
Citoyenne.* Even the word citizen rang male; you made the word
feminine, your charter of rights, calling for an end to suppression and a
beginning

to equality, and for that—of course—the guillotine. Men begat a Reign
of Terror. *La Terreur* meant chopping off heads of those that dared
question the existing patriarchal structures. How stupid.

Losing a head never erased your ideas. Olympe de Gouge,
La Citoyenne de le Monde, your cause is alive and thriving.
Havoc remains.

A CHANGE OF LEADERSHIP

JENNIFER MITCHELL

Decades have passed as I lift my sign again.
Progress slips away and rage builds in me.
Red rules sought to control my body.
Through ancient text dictated from their deity.
Used to decide my moral actions.
They twist the laws to fit their agenda.
Penalizing any domino involved.
Justitia is gripping her sword tighter.
Her scales forced to tilt backwards in time.
She is reduced to an incubator.
Transformed from human to machine.
Mandated to grow unwanted cells.
Legalized removal of her human freedom.
Only green protects the privileged.
The fight for rights and opportunity continues.
I pull my grey hair back and pass the baton to my little sisters.

WHAT'S LEFT

REBECCA CUTHBERT

My sister ran a pink plastic comb through her hair, long and straight as the water rushing from the high faucet in front of her. We stood in a campground bathroom, and outside, the sky had turned from periwinkle to violet. At eight years old, Kristin was weary of me, two and a half years younger. I was her burden and her shadow.

She moved with efficiency, then and always, wetting her comb and pulling it scalp to shoulder—the lawyer she'd one day be revealed in her quick, calculated movements. Behind her, I was all scabbed knees and bruised elbows.

* * *

My sister has two little girls. Their names are Mary Katherine and Abigail. Mary Katherine will be eight in the fall. Abigail just turned five. Mary Katherine has my first name for her middle; Abigail has my mother's—Marilyn. Mary Katherine is slim and precise. She enunciates clearly and uses punctuation when she texts me from my sister's phone. Abigail is ruled by emotion—angered by small injustices, thrilled by small generosities. They love each other ferociously.

Abigail and I both call our older sisters "Sissy," or the shorter "Sis." Kristin and Mary Katherine call us abbreviated versions of our own names, except for when they're sick of us.

* * *

There in the bathroom at the Penetanguishene campground, I watched moths flutter to a cracked light fixture and singe their wings on the bulb inside, pinging back to hit plastic. I saw them double in the dusty mirror, attracted to the light, rebuffed by the heat, again and again. My trance broke when I saw movement lower in the mirror.

228

Kristin's image twisted, left then right, checking her hair for snarls. Satisfied, she slid her comb into her back pocket and turned to leave.

"Wait for me!" I called, would always call, after her, but even as the words left my mouth, the heavy steel door was already clunking back into place. I didn't try to follow then; I wasn't finished. I picked up my toothbrush from the counter, wet it in the running faucet, and squeezed too much blue toothpaste onto it from the tiny tube Kristin left for me. I watched the moths again until I had to balance on my tiptoes to spit into the sink and rinse my toothbrush.

* * *

As adults, Kristin and I decided it was time to learn how to make and preserve jam, like our mother did with her mother. We swarmed the black raspberry bushes growing unchecked in our father's yard and picked them clean, holding ice packs to the bleeding scratches we earned. Then we took over the kitchen and stained its surfaces purple, using an old potato masher to crush berries in our mother's vintage Pyrex bowls.

My sister measures. I stir. Our jam is delicious. We made it every summer until 2020, when COVID ruined our plans and everyone else's. But my dad and I picked that year, anyway, freezing the berries for when Kristin could come home.

* * *

That long-ago night, the bathroom taps were too high, and I couldn't turn off the water. I left it running and used the toilet in the last stall. Concrete on two sides made it feel the most private, though I was alone in the bathroom, anyway. After I'd finished, I flicked my fingertips into the icy water, but couldn't reach the soap or paper towel dispenser. I wiped my hands on the dirty seat of my purple shorts and stuffed the toothpaste into my sweatshirt pocket. Then I picked up my toothbrush and tried to leave, to return to our green and white pop-up camper full of parents and siblings.

I couldn't open the door. I tried again, grunting, but it was too heavy for my chubby, useless arms. Next, I threw my shoulder into it, the soles of my flip flops squeaking on the worn-shiny cement floor. I turned around and heaved against it with my back, the pressure there blooming into a tender bruise I would feel for days. The door gave an inch, then creaked shut, mocking me. I was trapped. Defeated, I slid down its cold surface, scratched with graffitied words I was too young to know. I folded my arms over my banged-up knees, dropped my heavy head, and cried. The yellow fluorescent lights above me flickered and hummed.

* * *

Kristin and I branched out in 2019, visiting a local u-pick berry farm with her husband and girls. Mary Katherine diligently picked the fattest strawberries. Abigail plunked some into her cardboard box and ate just as many. After they ran off to play in the grassy aisle between crops with their dad, Kristin and I picked on, sweating in the July sunshine.

Later, Kristin and Mary Katherine and I sat around my kitchen table, picking off strawberry stems and adding the berries to a large metal colander. Abigail popped into the room every few minutes to eat the strawberries we deemed too small to bother with. We made dozens of jam puns, laughing until our stomachs hurt while our husbands rolled their eyes.

My favorite smell is simmering jam. My favorite sound is my sister's laugh.

* * *

Stuck in the campground bathroom, I didn't know how I would ever be found. I pictured my family packing up the camper, collapsing its roof, turning the hand crank until its sides pulled into its base. They'd attach it to my father's rusting Chevy and connect the trailer lights, then pull onto the highway and head home to Western New York. I didn't think they'd notice one child missing from the crowded station wagon.

Two or twenty minutes later, having spent most of my sobs, I peeked out from beneath my messy nest of brown curls for a quick survey of my prison. I saw chipped wall tiles and dirty grout. A daddy long legs perched in a corner. There was nowhere for me to sleep. I wondered if I could eat toothpaste if I got hungry. I took comfort in having toilets to use; I wasn't a baby anymore and would be ashamed of an accident. I wiped my nose on the back of my hand, noticing the blank smear it left in the dirt there. The faucet kept up its steady shushing flow, and the moths continued their suicide dance.

* * *

My sister and I collect vintage Pyrex. Her pattern is Spring Blossom, 70s green with white flowers, sometimes called "Crazy Daisy." Mine is Butterprint—turquoise, from the 50s, it's full of stylized roosters and farmers and piles of hay. We are experts at finding the mixing bowls and casserole dishes at yard sales and flea markets. Kristin has taught Mary Katherine and Abigail to spot Pyrex among tag sale jumbles, too. Someday, we hope the girls will choose their own patterns to collect.

My mother's bowls—a wedding gift in 1969—are still in the cupboard in the house where we grew up. They are a mix of greens and yellows from the Verde and Orange Daisy sets. Dad keeps them on a high shelf, but gets them for us when we visit. Once, when I asked him to "reach me down Mom's mixing bowls," he muttered that I sounded just like her. Something about Cheektowaga syntax. My sister and I laughed.

* * *

Sitting against the bathroom door that night, I felt something shift behind me, then an emptiness as it opened. I couldn't get up fast enough and fell back, smacking my tailbone. The quick pain trapped air in my chest. I squirmed sideways into a crouch and looked up. It was my mother.

I ran headfirst into her thighs, clutching the backs of her denimed legs. I breathed, I cried. I tried to explain, about the door, about my plan to eat toothpaste. I asked how they could leave me. I screamed "Don't you love me?!"

Four short years later, she died. I don't know what kind of memory the bathroom scene would have been for her.

* * *

Kristin plays 80s ballads in the car with her daughters. They all sing along. When I visit them, I sing too. Abigail often requests Boston's "Amanda." They also love "Africa" by Toto. Kristin and I try to hit the high notes in "Crocodile Rock" by Elton John. We fail. She and I are terrible singers.

* * *

That night in the bathroom, my mother picked me up to carry me, holding onto me with both arms. I clutched my toothbrush in a desperate fist and squeezed my eyes shut. She hadn't noticed the faucet running and I forgot to tell her.

She set me down when we reached our campsite. I turned and there was Kristin, standing outside the door of the camper, waiting for me in the fading light.

WHAT I WISHED

TESSA SWACKHAMMER

my friend's sister's cousin on their father's side had
a baby
and she named her Bailey and said she was a beauty
her nails as small as crescent moons
pressed to her palms so tightly they almost fused
and her mom told us to make a wish for baby Bailey
told us to think of something nice, something sweet,
but all I could think was what I wished
didn't happen to me

to baby Bailey I wish:
that you only know pain like
wanting to swim and having to wait for the rain
and
biking all the way to the store just to find you've forgotten your change
and
watching the backs of your friends on the sidewalk because you always
seem to fall
behind
and I wish that you only remember pain like
pants torn at the knee and hot summer days with muggy air and
bees stinging at your heels
because you might - be sad but
that's not the worst you could be
and maybe you fail a test or catch a cold on
the night of a movie you so desperately want to see
and maybe you'll make some enemies but
that's not the worst you could do
it's not the worst you could do.

I am telling you bad things will happen even if you don't want them to
but I hope it's never so bad that you think life isn't for you—
little, Baby Bailey

with the tiny crescent
moons
I can see your life mapped out in the stars and
in the walls of your little lavender room
and I hope that you stay young long enough
to keep believing in the possibility
of everything
and you're spared people like him and
agony like mine

I hope your life is the ache of adventure and the following of dreams
and
the only pain you ever have to know is the
gentle, kissing bite
of bee stings

ALPHABETICAL DISORDER

AMY BARNES

My son is born with a plastic spoon in his mouth. Not silver. When I'm cut open with a can opener after days of labor, it leaves a slash mark against my metal belly. I can see letters sloshing in my child with his first cry—a bellyfull bowlfull of alphabet soup letters and alphabet cereal.

I'm happy to see the alphabet inside of him. It means I was a good woman, a good mother who transmitted baby book worthy words: whispered stories, sing-song lyrics, math problems and science facts, nursery rhymes with the scary parts about falling out of tall mommy trees censored. It almost made up for the Dr. Pepper and Sonic cheeseburgers and pregnant vomit word cussing.

When he is born, my umbilical words have nearly choked him. He arrives not speaking and not breathing, gripping his throat with tiny fingers trying to speak so I know he is okay and doesn't need help. A man named *A for Apgar,* and not *H for Heimlic*h rates my child: *5 for fail. f for fail.* The letters squeeze my son's veins and blood until he is the color of weak tomato broth with letters floating under his thin skin. Letters line-up in his chart and nurses and doctors scrawl notes in letters I can't read, don't want to read, can't say out loud.

* * *

At home, I secretly pry his baby mouth open to try and force words. Any words. Any sounds. I push his perfect bow lips together to form the *mmmm* sound for mom. It's a guttural sound that calls me and one only I understand. I treasure the sound. I become a skilled codewalker codemother interpreting needs and wants and commands and complaints. I watch the "m" vibrate in his throat. *My* letter. The *mom* letter. It's all buried next to *eplitogottis* that he can't say either.

I reach deep and pull spit-covered letters out of his throat to lay out, as simple *examples*.

Dog
Cat
Mom
Dad
Hat
Sat

He puts them back in his mouth and swallows them all before I can stop him.

* * *

The baby books say *developmentally* (I say that with conviction and faith and table-pounding urgency to strangers and strange doctors with long titles,) he should be talking.

Occasionally, he belches out words, mixed-up letters, Basil E. Frankweiller-level files of backwards letters and stuck-together-wrongness. Baby babble becomes toddler entanglements becomes almost-kindergarten word chaos. We continue talking in code, mother and son like people at war sending secret messages. The plastic primary colored communication works but only for us, not for other kids or other parents or other people without a throat full of letters.

I dig in the backyard and park yards and parks for a Rosetta Stone to translate. He helps me search and we lay out rocks in rows next to cars in rows and plastic dogs in rows and army men in battle rows. I look for a base language to start with.

As we wait for the weighty words to arrive, I trek with him to libraries and playgroups with heavy backpacks of metal printing press font and stop sign letters and advertisement sign fonts.

* * *

I find a woman with words to spare, for $100 an hour. She lays them out in new translations. My son lick-reads the words, lickety-split, banana-split. Somehow the words are tattooed on his tongue, renting space like car race word sponsors. This woman magician has all the speech runes in her pockets. She tosses them on the table.

236

D - O – G

Three wet Alpha-Bit letter bits fly out of my son's mouth, disordered, and reordered in no order.

Dogdogdogdogdogdogdog

The d's and the g's and the o's roll, clank against each other in the cartoon bubble over his head, filling it full with letter jumbles. The word is heavy and important. One syllable. His tongue clacks against his teeth like metal spoons in a jug band.

Abracadabra

The woman with rune stones and word stones opens and reopens his face mouth door with a wave. She tells *me* I've given him a *fricate* of a name that is almost impossible to say. I mouth *I m sorry* to her and to him and to the world as the word scramble of a's and b's and c's create a floodgate of stored-up stomach words, magnetic letters, a clanky printmaker's alphabet, sentences and structure, formed and joined and finally born again.

TREAT

There he is, just like I knew he would be, arms in the freezer and rosy cheeks, stocking merchandise. He looks just as adorable as he does every time—skinny black jeans, a hoodie, all those gangly limbs. He's wearing a beanie even though it's the middle of summer, and his shaggy brown hair sneaks out from underneath. I don't know his name—I imagine it's Matthew or Jacob, something generic and youthful—but today is the day I'll find out.

I'm wearing my most sexy-yet-casual outfit—leggings tight in all the right places, t-shirt with just enough cleavage showing that he might be tempted to look. My hair is done but not too done. I don't want to look like I'm trying, just naturally beautiful, which is the most difficult type of beauty to capture. I don't know if that's his type, but I imagine it is.

"I'm going to run some errands," I told my husband, yelled through the crack in his office door. He was inside hard at work and did not want to be interrupted. Part of me didn't want him to see me all dolled up for the grocery store, how desperate I would look. Would he suspect, feel a jealousy percolating just below the surface? Would he even notice?

I don't need blueberries, but he is standing in front of the blueberries, so now I need them. As I approach, I clench my muscles and toss my hair and queue up my smile for the moment when he notices me. I am a treat for him, I tell myself. He spends all day doing menial labor, stocking shelves, fingertips freezing. I will make his day, however subtly, and this in turn will make my own.

I stop next to him, keeping my eyes on the freezer though I watch him distinctly out of my peripheral vision.

"Hey," I say. "Mind if I take one of those off your hands?"

He doesn't acknowledge me, just continues to toss ice-encrusted bags from the box in his hands onto the freezer rack.

"Can I have one of those?" I repeat, louder this time.

He finally looks at me, sending a tingle of satisfaction through my limbs. His mouth hangs open, those full pink lips that I imagine grinding between my teeth, and he reaches up to rip out headphones that I hadn't noticed snaking out from his beanie.

"What was that?" he asks. His voice is like honey, freshly deep just a few years out from puberty.

I give him a measured smile, displaying none of the giddiness bouncing around in my chest, and point. "Mind if I grab one of those from you?"

His eyes flick down, and he hands me the bag. As I take it, my fingertips brush his. They are cold from the freezer, and I imagine the heat of mine melting dots of warmth on his red skin, a mark of my presence.

"There ya go," he says quickly. His eyes are already back in the freezer, his other hand already back in the box, going for the next bag, his awareness out of my reach. The headphones bounce against his chest, the muffled, percussive sound of either punk rock or rap before he begins to stuff them back in his ears.

I have to say something, grasp for the string of his attention.

"Are these ones on sale?" I ask.

"Uhhh…" He leans back, scanning the shelves. "Forton Valley? Yeah, dollar off it looks like."

"Oh, great!" I say with maybe too much enthusiasm.

"Yeah, good deal." He goes for the headphones again, so I continue.

"Have you had these before?"

He raises his eyebrows. "Have I had blueberries before?"

"I mean, these ones," I clarify. "This Forton Valley? Is this a good brand?"

He shrugs, tosses a bag onto the shelf. "Sure, I guess. We sell a lot of them."

My skin flushes despite goosebumps from the chill of the open door rising on my forearms. I must press, keep this momentum.

"Could you possibly tell me where the...the wine is located?"

"Wine's in aisle eight," he answers flatly.

"But there's this specific brand that I'm looking for. Could you help me find it?"

He stuffs the headphones in his pocket and tosses the box of blueberries onto a cart behind him where they clatter against the metal. "Uh, yeah, I can try."

My heart beats madly as I follow him toward aisle eight, where I know very well the wine is located. A bead of sweat rolls between my breasts, but I maintain my cool. I remind myself that I have no reason to be nervous. I am a treat. I watch his skinny legs, the awkward gait, the touchstone slouch of his shoulders that I imagine taper to a thin, pasty waist, jutting hip bones and the soft dip of a belly button. So delicate I could break him, and he would love every second of it.

"What kind of wine is it?" he asks as we near the wall of glittering bottles. I wonder if he has ever even tasted wine.

"A pinot noir. The brand was Gillian." I pause to smirk. "Gillian's my name, so it stuck in my mind."

I'm making this shit up, this fake brand name, the same as my own.

He sets his hands on his hips and scans the shelf. I know he's not really looking, just giving the illusion of it, and I feel the tiniest bit guilty. I don't even like wine. When I could drink, I preferred a full-bodied scotch, something that would stick to my teeth.

"I can go ask my manager, I guess," he says, still not making eye contact. I know he's hoping that I'll let it go, just pick something else and go.

"Oh, no, you don't have to do that. I'll just get...this." I reach out and grab the bottle closest to me, a purpley-black malbec. "You ever had this one?"

He rubs his chin, a nervous habit perhaps, running chewed nails through his minimal scatter of a beard. "I...uh...no, not a big wine-drinker."

Please think I'm cool. Please think I'm young.

"Well, it looks tasty. I'll take it."

He smiles, noticeably relieved. "Sorry about the other one. I just stock food and stuff, so I don't really know—"

I lay my hand on his shoulder. The soft, warm knob of it stiffens beneath my hand and I give it a gentle squeeze, subtle enough that maybe he imagined it, maybe he hoped for it. Maybe it's just enough, along with the tight pants and the tousled hair and the saccharine sweetness, to kickstart the spiral of his mind, unwind his curiosity until it converges with mine.

"Thank you for your help. I didn't catch your name?"

His lips curl into a bashful smile, a dimple sinking into his cheek. "It's, uh—it's Christopher."

Christopher. I chew on the syllables, working the meaty heft of the name around my tongue, squeezing breath between the sounds.

"Christopher," I repeat. "Thanks, Christopher."

"No problem." He reaches into his pocket, rooting around for the headphones as he turns to go back to the freezer. I watch him walk away, working them into his ears, eyes on the linoleum, his black skater shoes thunking with each step.

The malbec is sweaty in my hands as I carefully place it back on the shelf.

* * *

That night, up in bed while my husband sleeps on the couch downstairs, I masturbate furiously thinking about Christopher.

I don't think about us fucking. I don't picture him above me, his skinny arms in my peripheral vision, clammy skin sliding against mine, the feeling of fucking someone who doesn't feel like he is owed my body. Instead, I picture him with somebody else, some faceless, pretty college girl. His friend's roommate or his lab partner or some girl he met at a party. I watch from the outside, see him seduce her, run his hands over her eager, supple body and whisper things in her ear that I can't hear. I watch her take off the layers of his clothes—unzip the hoodie, undo the belt, remove the beanie from his head—and press herself against his pale skin. I don't know if I want to be her or if I just want to witness sex being spontaneous and joyful, the kind of sex you have when you are young, when enthusiasm supersedes duty, and you have to rush before it slips away.

When I come, my belly vibrates with a pulsing thrum, cracking open a wide, indescribable void I can fall into. An escape.

* * *

You didn't get creamer," my husband grumbles with his back to me in the kitchen the next morning.

I am at the table eating plain dry toast with one hand—the only thing I can stomach anymore—and scrolling mindlessly through Instagram with the other. My ears perk up, sensing opportunity like a dog hearing the rattle of a leash.

"Oh shit, I totally forgot," I feign. I do this on purpose. Always forget one thing. Don't get enough. Pour milk down the drain or hide toilet paper rolls in my car. Make reasons to go back. "I'll stop and get some today."

My husband sighs theatrically. "You wouldn't have to go to the store every fucking day if you could just remember these things. Is it really that hard?"

If you want to bitch about the fucking shopping, how about you do it for once? is what I want to say. But I hold back. I stuff the rest of the toast in my mouth, its edges cutting up the fragile insides of my cheeks. I silently get up, grab my keys, and slam the door harder than necessary behind me.

* * *

Christopher isn't there today. I go up and down the aisles, circle back over and over again, but he is nowhere to be found. The disappointment sours my mood, but I try to be reasonable. He must have days off, right? I wonder why he didn't tell me, then I remember there is no reason he would. He doesn't even know my name.

I get the creamer I came for and other random things to make the trip worthwhile. French bread, a hunk of smoked cheese, some grapefruit. I grab the Forton Valley blueberries just because, then find myself in front of the wine. I see the malbec from yesterday, set slightly askew like I'd left it. It's smooth and cold as I run my fingertips over the glass. I try to recall the taste, cloying, that cloying black-cherry richness that coats your mouth. I consider buying it, until I remember that I can't drink, and my anger boils.

On my way home, I take the long, unnecessary route, looping past the city pool and the Catholic cemetery, down the length of Main street and back up again. I do this more often than I'd ever admit. I know when I'm a mother I won't be able to do ridiculous things like this, that I'll never again have the opportunity to waste time or be alone. But right now, I feel a constant, egging loneliness that swells and undulates like oceanic waves, begging for anything to dispel the agitation.

As I'm turning around in a bank parking lot, rain begins to fall. It hits suddenly, the sky blackening in an instant as thunder rumbles out of the bruise of clouds. I pull out into the street. The wipers can't go fast enough—even at the highest speed, everything is a blur, but I refuse to slow down. The thrill of danger soothes me in a way, feeds my hunger for excitement.

I see a dark shape as I crest a hill, walking along the sidewalk with a gait I'd recognize anywhere. The skinny legs, the downcast gaze, the beanie. My throat catches and I think that it must be a mirage, a hallucination born of my whole delusional morning, yet I pull violently to the side of the road, casting water up over the curb. He looks at me as I roll down the window.

"Christopher?" I yell through the roar of the storm.

He stares, eyes squinting into the rain, and cautiously steps closer. "Yeah?"

"It's Gillian. From the grocery store."

His mouth hangs open in confusion. The moment is interminable, and I think how ridiculous this must seem.

"Do you want a ride?" I finally yell.

He looks up and down the street, as if a better option might pull up behind me, and tosses his hands up. "Sure."

He gets in and slams the door, and he's in my car. Christopher is in my car. Him and I, the grocery store boy and me. With the noise of the rain and the blur of it on the windows, the seclusion feels even more complete.

"Thanks," he mutters. "That rain is brutal."

He runs a hand over his face, wipes the rain away, leaving his skin dewy and clean. His lip bounces as his hand sweeps over it, and my heart somersaults in my throat.

"No problem at all," I reply, calm, collected, concealing my excitement. I tear my eyes away from him, look out the rearview, pull onto the road. "Where are you headed?"

"Just back to my apartment. Down by the university."

From where from where from where, I want to ask. From a girlfriend's house? Did he stay the night? Did they fuck last night, maybe this morning? Is that what that glow in his cheeks is from? The thought makes me want to gobble him up.

"You go to the university?" I ask.

He shakes his head, sending little splatters of water everywhere. "No, I just live down there."

I nod. "Do you always walk? Like, for transportation?"

"Yeah, I guess."

Why? Where is your car? Is it getting worked on? Did you get in an accident? Was it your fault or theirs? Did you drop everything, get rid of all your belongings, move across the country to this tiny college town to work at the grocery store? Were you fleeing a bad family, a bad relationship, a bad reputation?

I come over another hill and down Main Street for the third or fourth time today. Christopher is quiet, fiddling with the strings on his hoodie. His body is tensed, as if he is afraid to touch any part of my car. The university district is on the other side of downtown, old brick buildings nestled up against the riverfront. Apartments pepper the neighborhood, one of which must be where he lives, and my panic bubbles knowing that this serendipitous moment together will soon end.

I have to draw it out. I must think of some excuse, some diversion, some way to stretch time and keep him in my grasp.

"Listen, I have to run a quick errand while we're in the neighborhood," I say. "Is that okay? Are you in a hurry?"

He shakes his head. "No, that's fine. Go for it."

I smile, relief washing through me. "Thanks, Chris. That's really sweet of you. Do you mind? If I call you Chris?" It feels sweetly dangerous, going out on a limb.

He shrugs again, as if indifference is the only response in his repertoire. "Yeah, sure."

I glance around the streets. The sidewalks have cleared out, everyone escaping the rain inside. I see a parking spot along the curb and pull in.

"It'll be really quick, I promise." I touch his arm. "Thank you *so* much."

He tenses under my hand, but again shrugs and shakes his head like nothing matters to him. "Yeah, no biggie. It's cool."

I deploy the plump, flirtatious smile I perfected when I was young, that I'd especially concocted in order to commandeer the attention of men. I haven't used it in years. "I'll be right back."

Outside, the rain is deafening. I throw my arms over my head but am soaked instantly. I run into the first door I see. It's one of those hipster vintage boutiques that sells overpriced used clothing and has some snappy, feminine name. Old-school Madonna is pumping through the speakers and I suddenly feel my age calcifying within me.

"Hey-ey," says a sing-song voice as a girl pops out from behind the counter. She's tiny and adorable, manic-pixie-dream-girl style. Huge doll-eyes behind thick-rimmed glasses, blunt bangs, sharp porcelain collar bones peaking out of her sweater. I feel a gut punch of envy. "Welcome to Clementine's! Looking for anything in particular?"

I take a deep breath and wait for the whiplash of my emotions to settle. I couldn't imagine what I'd be looking for here, a place so impossibly cool that it nearly repels me. "Nothing in particular, thank you."

She smiles sweetly. There's a tiny gap between her front teeth, a perfect God-given imperfection. "No biggie! Let me know if you need help."

No biggie. What is this language they share? Is this the dialect of youth, this communal informality, something I'm too jaded to tap into? Or do these two have a more specific connection? Could this be the girlfriend whose house he was coming from, the one he fucks in my dreams?

Now that I've imagined it, it becomes real, and suddenly I'm sick with jealousy. Of course he would go for her, with her fragile petite figure, her sweet but self-righteous attitude. I'm sure she is fun and carefree, makes witty jokes and gets every pop culture reference. I bet she can roll a perfect joint and gives good head. They probably watch obscure foreign films together and fuck on her couch. I bet he

245

tells her she's beautiful and she scrunches up her button nose as she laughs at him. I bet he kisses her along her pearly collar bones and she tells him it tickles. I bet he is in love with her.

"You know..." I say. "Now that you mention it, I *am* looking for something."

The girl turns back from the jewelry display and grins. "What can I help you find?"

I think about Chris in my car out front, and my body pulses with heat.

"I want to look young."

I half-expect her to laugh in my face—*look at this old bitch, this mother, she wants to look young* —but instead she claps her hands together, her purple nails flashing.

"I know *just* the thing."

* * *

The rain hasn't abated when I make my way back out to the car, but it's lessened enough that I don't have to run. I realize as I approach that the engine is still humming, that Christopher could have driven away with my car if he wanted to.

"Sorry that took so long," I say as I get in, all breathy and fake-winded,. "You good in here?"

He leans into his elbow against the window, fingers digging into his hair. His eyes are sleepy, weighed down by his abundance of eyelashes, and his glance sends an electric surge down my spine.

"Yeah, I'm good. Did you, uh, get your errand done?"

I run my tongue over my lips, freshly painted with the lipstick that the Clementine's girl picked out for me. The shade is a fresh, visceral pink, vaginal, like a slick organ. I subtly bite my lip, tasting its sweet chemical flavor. I hope he notices the lipstick but doesn't. I want him not to see the difference, but to realize that I was beautiful all along. *I am a treat*, I repeat to myself, fingering the tube in my pocket, remembering the feeling as the Clementine's girl helped me apply it, holding my chin delicately in her lithe fingers, her gap-toothed mouth just inches from mine.

I pull into traffic, grasping for my next move in my head.

How long have you worked at the grocery store?"

Christopher rubs his chin and I feel the phantom scratch of his stubble on my fingertips. "Since I moved here in June."

Of course, I know this.

"What brings you to town?"

He works his lip between his teeth, contemplating his answer. "Just looking for something new, I guess. Maybe I'll go to the university one of these days. We'll see."

He's being vague, evasive. I can sense the tension in his voice, the past that he's trying to hide, the textured background story that I've imagined for him.

"I remember when I first moved here," I replied. "I had just finished undergrad upstate and had no idea what to do next. Do I go to grad school? Find a job? Do I move back home?"

He nods slowly, still watching the rain. Is he even listening? Keep pushing.

"It's scary to be in a new place. I didn't know anyone, and it was so hard to meet people. It can be so fucking lonely, right?"

Is the vulnerability too much? Is the swearing too much? I want him to feel comfortable around me, to come off as cool and chill, easy to talk to.

"Yeah, for sure." He shifts his weight and pulls his phone from his pocket. My heart rate increases, rage igniting, as I imagine the text he is sending right now to the Clementine's girl. *Got a ride from this weird random lady and she won t stop talking. Can t wait to see you tonight. Let s fuck.*

"Hey, are you in a rush or anything?" I ask.

He glances up. "I mean, not really, but—"

"I was thinking," I interrupt, bypassing my mental filter, spitting it out before my better judgment can stop me. "I was thinking of maybe stopping for a drink? There's this pub by the riverfront that I love. What do you think? Would you like that?"

His eyes grow dinner-plate big, shockingly big, and he suddenly looks more childlike than I'd like him to.

"I...I dunno, I should probably be headed home..."

I don't let myself stop. If I slow down enough to let my own ridiculous words or his apprehension settle in, I will die of shame.

"It won't be for long. Just a quick one, I promise."

"I mean, I'm twenty. I can't even order a drink."

247

"Don't worry about that. I'll buy for you, obviously. Don't you think it'd be fun? Just to talk, get to know each other a little better."

His chest recedes and I realize he's been holding his breath. "You don't have to do that..."

I pick up his scent—weed and cinnamon gum and saliva—and the urge to kiss him is nearly undeniable. How do I not eat him alive?

"It'd be my pleasure, believe me. My treat. Just one drink."

"It's, like, 10AM."

"Come on, I know you want to, Christopher. A treat. Don't you think you deserve a treat?"

I'm buzzing. My heart beats so fucking hard, so fast, hummingbird wings wild inside my chest, pulsing through the entire cavity of my torso. I no longer care what I look like, what I sound like, maniacal and desperate, a writhing animal, and I can only obey the motion of my desires.

"I just want a ride home."

"I don't think that's all you want, Chris."

"What are you talking—"

"Chris, I am extremely attracted to you."

It's a last-ditch effort. I am hollow, in desperate need of being filled.

"Whoa, okay, I don't think—"

Push. Push. Push.

"And I just want to—"

"Whoa whoa whoa!"

The crunch of metal and the whoosh of the airbag and the force of being smashed against it happens in a hysterical fraction of a second. Diamonds of glass rain down on us, blasted from the obliterated windshield, and the coppery wetness of blood dribbles into my eyes.

They say your life flashes before your eyes in times like this, but it's less like my life and more like my mistakes, all the minuscule actions that add up to foolish disasters. It's a laundry list of all the apologies I'll have to make, populating like rolling credits on the black insides of my eyelids.

How will I explain this? I ask myself as I wait for the cops to come, for the ambulance to arrive, for my husband to rescue me from my recklessness, while Christopher sits on the curb, silent and horrified, with blood trickling down his face.

In the end, I'll explain it as exactly what it is—I gave a boy a ride home in the rain.

* * *

Time passes. The stitches in my forehead get removed. The gash fades to a scar. We get a new vehicle, and our insurance goes through the roof. My belly swells and shakes with the life growing inside of it, undeniable now, and then the baby comes, and nothing has ever felt more real. My days fill with nursing and playgroups and pediatrician appointments, with tummy time and sleep training. The baby I never wanted becomes the sole focus of my attention.

Motherhood is the ultimate clarifying event, a mass reprioritizing of my scattered life, my flailing brain. All the distractions fall away, boughs trimmed from the branches of my existence, to reveal my core and its incomprehensible ability to be content.

One night, my husband suggests dinner at a restaurant downtown. A celebration of sorts—Cora turned a year-old last week, and I successfully renewed my teaching license. He's a different man now, or we recognize each other in a different way. Maybe he developed a new appreciation when my life was threatened in the accident. Or maybe when he saw his wife turn into a mother, his love deepened in the way nature intended. It doesn't matter. It's one of those peaceful nights where everything is serene and smooth—Cora with a giant pink bow on her head, my husband with his hand lightly on my thigh. I am impossibly happy.

I sip on a foamy microbrew, tipsy after only half a glass. My husband and I talk about our bathroom remodel and his upcoming work presentation and when we will take Cora to the zoo, all the simple minutiae of our simple life. Cushy familiar things that I can settle into, that wrap me up like a blanket so that I can feel myself breathe.

I'm leaning over to pick up Cora's sippy cup from the floor for the thousandth time when our waiter approaches.

"Hey, I'm Christopher, and I'll be taking care of you guys tonight."

My stomach lurches, a surge of warmth that hasn't felt familiar in so long. That honey-rich voice dribbling over thick lips. I look up and my fear and desire are confirmed.

I'm shocked to see that his hair, those thick brown curls that I fantasized about running between my fingers, is shorn into a close-crop. In his black waiter's uniform and shiny shoes, he looks clean-cut and mature. He looks like a man. His eyes are still so enormous I could lose myself in them, and a jagged pink scar runs along his temple, shiny fragile skin that matches my own.

"Another beer for you, ma'am?"

When he addresses me, he looks me straight in the eye. There is no fear, no apprehension, and absolutely no recognition. Maybe he erased me from his memory, wiped away the trauma as his own form of self-preservation, or maybe with my husband and my baby, I'm just another woman. I am no one special. I wonder for a second if I imagined it all, if the loneliness and the obsession and Christopher himself were just a dream, then I bring my hand to my face, run my fingers across the scar snaking down my forehead, evidence of my infatuation. A reminder that the past, all the iterations of myself, were once real.

"Well, *I'll* take another. The stout, please," my husband chimes in after I've been silent long enough.

Christopher smiles and walks away. I watch his stride as he crosses the restaurant, confident and purposeful, no slumped shoulders or averted gaze. He's a different iteration of himself too.

My husband squeezes my shoulder. "You okay?"

Like a gut punch of instinct, I immediately consider getting up to find him. Wander the restaurant, look up and down the bar, walk straight back into the fucking kitchen and bang pots and pans until he recognizes me. I feel the old hum of being drawn toward him, the desire to manifest my fantastical imagination, but then Cora emits a cry, reaching for her sippy cup, and I'm pulled back into reality.

"Yeah, I'm fine," I reply as I push my glass away. "Too much beer, I think."

* * *

I bumble my way through dinner. I strategically take Cora to
get her diaper changed when Christopher returns, and my husband
orders for me. When he comes back to ask how everything tastes, I
smile flatly and don't make eye contact, and when he brings the check,
I'm already walking out to the car, Cora having grown tired and whiny.

The car ride home is peaceful. As the sunset blows the sky
apart, Cora snoozes in her carseat, and my husband holds my hand. He
kisses my fingers and I know it should feel like love.

I carry Cora into the house and tuck her into her crib, running
my fingers over her curls and cheeks and perfect tiny ears. Her
eyelashes flutter and I feel the acceleration of my heart settle, my
adrenaline slipping away. I breathe in and out the milky, lavender scent
of the nursery. I lay down next to my husband, feel the heft of his arm
over my body. I close my eyes.

I see him in my dreams, where the impossible iterations of
ourselves seek refuge between the softness of imagination and a hard,
unrelenting reality.

Will this be enough?

A MOTHER'S LOVE IS SAND IN A SIEVE

CHRISTINE NAPRAVA

Stupid,
stupid,
idiot
was the daughter with the frosted, feathered hair
who downed too many fruity drinks at a forgettable bar
and vomited the sunset beside the cracked concrete pad in the backyard
of the house that could've been huffed, puffed, and blown away
by any wolf, large or small, steel-lunged or asthmatic.
Mother Hawk had never known excess—
she had resisted Drink,
she had wed First and Only Boyfriend,
she had trusted Husband,
she had borne Stupid, Stupid, Idiot Mistake Daughter
who now bit back and filled out her clothes in ways pleasurable to men.
You had your fun and now look at you.
Mother Hawk locked the back door,
ignoring the gaping kitchen window,
forgetting that Stupid, Stupid, Idiot Daughter was taller, smarter.
Mother Hawk went to bed,
night-daydreaming of Farm,
of Stupid, Stupid, Idiot Sister and snoring,
of suffocating,
of Hershey chocolate bars for Christmas,
of dresser drawers of defiled, sharp-smelling rags.
Mother Hawk drifted with her ears keen to a ruckus in the kitchen,
the dish drying rack clattering against the linoleum,
only neither ever ensued.
Stupid, Stupid, Idiot Daughter ventured off,
empty stomach,
stinging windpipe,
in search of a mother
and found a husband instead.

DOXOLOGY

LINDSEY HEATHERLY

Praise God, from whom all blessings flow;
Praise him, all creatures here below;
Praise him above, ye heavenly hosts;
Praise Father, Son, and Holy Ghost. Amen.

Thomas Ken, 1674

Six months pregnant. Twenty years old.

Blue maternity shirt. The only one that fits through the entire pregnancy.

Shuffle down the pew aisle, in front of the family you used to know. The ones that took you to your first college football game and set up tailgating before the sun rose. The ones who put you to work dicing onions and green bell peppers for omelets under the tent in that parking lot on game day. The ones whose eldest son accompanied you to Junior Prom. The ones who looked to you as the responsible one, the eldest of five, the polite one, the kind one, the one who knew how to keep her mouth and legs closed.

Avert your eyes from theirs. Make eye contact with the red hymnals saluting the pulpit. Two verses into this hymn of five, or was it six?

Hold your breath as you walk to the front of the sanctuary and through the right door that leads to the back of the church, where Sunday School and Daycare take place.

Empty your lungs and your bladder in the tiny, porcelain white bathroom in the porcelain white church where you wore your porcelain white wedding dress four months prior. Try not to dirty the walls with your transgressions.

Listen for piano music, take a deep breath, and hold as you walk down the hall and out the door that leads back into the sanctuary to face the congregation. Walk down the same aisle, shuffle down the same pew. Ignore the young blonde with long hair, sitting beside the eldest son, drowning in department store perfume.

Pick up your copy of the red hymnal. Snap the book shut as the music stops and you take your seat. Ignore the hand that rests around your shoulder. The same hand that took yours in matrimony some months prior. Compare *matrimony* to *penance*. Ignore the stares from your right and focus on the cross above the preacher. Listen to the sermon being preached from the pulpit. Listen for hope. Listen for forgiveness. Shed silent tears.

When the sermon is over, sing the Doxology and close your eyes as the preacher gives the Benediction. Sing *Amen* three times, then cradle your bible and prepare for socializing.

Summon the courage to walk to the family to your right, the family who used to love you, and speak to the eldest son. Smile and extend your hand to the young blonde with long hair and heavy perfume, and marvel at the diamond on her finger. Congratulate them both and maintain eye contact, commanding their gazes away from your growing stomach.

Swallow and notice the lump in your throat as you say hello to other members of the congregation on the way out the front doors of the porcelain white church where you wore your porcelain white wedding dress four months prior.

Sit in your car and wait for your husband, chatting with the pastor, your father, the other family's father about football and college graduation plans. Swallow your shame until it bursts forth in tears streaming down your cheeks.

WHO PREPARED THE LAST SUPPER?

JODY RAE

No, but really, who?
Luke wrote
that Jesus sent Peter + John to go and prepare the Passover feast, but
who milled and bought the flour? Whose oil did they use?
Who mixed the flour with oil and salt? Who pressed the dough
and baked the bread?
Whose oven did they use?
Who harvested and treaded the grapes? Who fermented and stored
the wine?
Who set the table?
Who drew and hauled the water for their thirst and for their foot
washing?
It was the women, wasn't it?
Unseen or unwritten, blotted or edited out,
the unread women of the Last Supper mopped the floors
where washwater splashed,
where the wine spilled,
where the oil dripped.
Cloaked in invisibility and politics, the women cleared the table and
washed the dishes
and put them away.
Jesus surely saw them.
I'd like to tell them I can see them, too.

THE GOLDEN ASP

N.E. GRIFFIN

This asp's bite would not be fatal. The priestess had assured me of that. This asp bore in her icy veins a magic encoded in stone-carved glyphs, called forth by the priestess herself—a venom that gave life, rather than took it.

Indeed, the creature who emerged from the reed-woven basket with a peevish hiss bore only passing resemblance to those that slithered by the riverside. She was of similar size and shape, but her scales shimmered an uncanny gold, as if she were dressed for court. A royal asp, then. How fitting.

Her bite would not be an end, but a beginning. A chance to start my story afresh. To right those wrongs that could still be rectified.

Apart from the asp's susurrations, the mausoleum that had become my sanctuary remained silent. My slaves banished; my children sent away to ensure their safety from the army that stalked our palace gates. I raised my looking glass to regard my unqueenly visage, smeared with tears, kohl, and lover's blood—visible reminders of my grief. The sight brought tears anew. This was the portrait of defeat.

Perhaps I had chosen wrong. Perhaps I should send the golden asp away, demand instead a common asp or a vial of belladonna. It would be the honorable thing, some would say, to follow my beloved on his journey to the Underworld. Maybe this was where I was destined to end, a queen vanquished.

I swirled my wine in its chalice, contemplating the potency of poison and the chill silence of a grave. Death would be a relief, a kind of ecstatic freedom.

My heart pounded in my ears, protesting its desire to go on beating. The asp hissed in her basket, unwilling to be forgotten. She was sent here with a duty she meant to complete.

256

I too had responsibilities. To a people, loath to be subjugated. To royal children, who must not be humiliated. To my departed lover, whose memory demanded vengeance.

I grasped the asp's neck and extracted her from her basket. "Hush now, sweet serpent. Your time has come." She writhed with excitement.

Her teeth bit into flesh like a seamstress's needles. If this had been death, it would have been a nice one. No sword skewering my belly. No enraged, tearing mobs.

But it was not death. Instead of sleepy release, my body thrummed with elation. My limbs felt twice as strong, then thrice, and I knew how it must feel to be a warrior in the throes of battle. Omnipotent and invincible.

I picked up my beloved's still-bloody sword from the marble floor of the mausoleum. It felt light as linen. I wielded it as easily as he ever had, and I envied his years of soldiering, if this were the sensation. Whatever could have brought him to the shelter of my silks, if this was his life beyond the palace walls?

The crackle of oil lamps grew loud like the hammering of hail, the scent of incense as pungent as the stench of a funeral pyre.

The priestess had said the effects would be manifold, foretelling heightened strength and senses, as well as a faculty she called the snakesilver tongue. I stuck my tongue out, half expecting to see it forked.

Silly notion. It was a psychic transformation she had anticipated, not a physical one. I had always been cunning at charming men, but the snakesilver tongue would make my will indomitable. Armies that had once fled to our enemies would flock to my banner at the gentlest command. The people would cheer me from Iberia to Armenia. Poets would record the histories as I wished them remembered.

I smiled at my reflection, washing away the outward symbols of my grief before painting my eyes afresh. I stripped naked, discarding my finery on the floor. The asp's bite had already healed, and she hissed happily beside my fallen dress, her task complete.

I sorted through those adornments of soldiery my beloved and my boys had left behind. Some too large, others too small. I would need to have some pieces custom-made for me. But this sword, his

257

sword, I would keep as my own, its blade forever remembering the blood of its most princely victim.

From my erstwhile tomb, I would emerge. After the army at my gates was defeated, I would set sail upon a gilded barge towards a future where I would be remembered as history's greatest regent, honorably wed to a noble husband who had been betrayed by a duplicitous friend, a usurping tyrant. They would speak of me as a virtuous queen left with no choice but to take up arms in pursuit of justice.

History was written by the victor, after all.

THE PORTRAIT

JASMINA KUENZLI

I remember eyes that were a dark brown, with flecks of gold, and lips that were like a slash from a painter's brush, delicate in a face otherwise constructed of only sharp lines and edges

I remember joy in those eyes, a sadness that hid behind them like the sun hiding behind clouds.

I remember whispering because there was something between us that couldn't be named, arresting, and alluring and sudden, like the arrays of lightning that crackled across the sky, hitting us all at once, and setting my hair on end.

I remember wondering if all love would feel like this, standing in the middle of the tracks as a train hurtled down to collide, and refusing to let it sweep by like it was nothing.

I remember the curve of your smile like you knew something I didn't and the shape of your head beneath my hands, and how in that moment, I could feel us slipping away.

I remember the third space of phone calls, an interdimensional wormhole where my doubts were so often suspended, except when the silence brought them in, and how my voice became so choked with longing, it was a wonder you could not taste it in the air.

I remember a hand raised like a flag, and the rush of a red heart, and the heat that ran along my skin in the dark, lining my every movement in gold

And I still have your face imprinted behind my eyelids, like the afterimages of sunlight. I keep buying different looking glasses— books and stories and poetry and music, and still, when my eyes shut, it is only to see you behind them

Just like the letters I have memorized and the pauses between your words, and the harsh light of that shitty restaurant, where the waiter and I both knew what you didn't because you were too busy staring at your phone, waiting for her to call…

That night, you drove to her place. Did your heart sink when you saw his car there instead of yours?

Did you ever think of me, in my own bed, feeling you slipping away from me like water through my hands?

Did you ever remember that night when you cried to me on the phone, because I couldn't go into that space with you again, not when the world was falling down around us, not when the asphalt cracked in two and the Earth flooded?

I let you go in the middle of an apocalypse, but I still keep looking back for you.

Are you still waiting outside the house of someone who never saw you the way I did, like a decaying portrait?

I know what that feels like.

A pen to paper over and over again.

BRUSH STROKES ON CANVAS

JOANN KOOZER

Old woman feels the evening pull
   like the ebb tide,
she slowly drifts
    to her west window,
anticipating a broad splash of sunset

A day yawns,
sunrays and drifting particles
concoct one last batch of taffy

yellows and reds, blues
   kneaded and pulled across
     the dimming western sky,
       stretched and braided

Purples emerge, chase orange,
each one glows and glances off long yellow streaks,
pink edges try to soften red's dominance
in the final dip of this day's dance

Thirty-six thousand, one hundred thirty-five
unique sunsets chasing sunrises she has witnessed

At 99, ensconced
in comfortable rooms,
she and I (now the parent)
reminisce, play Skip-Bo or dominoes,

repeat, repeat every family story,
laugh at the same old chestnuts,
including ourselves,
fallen from the same sappy tree

Unsteady,
she bumps, bops, pokes,
leans a little too hard
against once-friendly furniture

Elbows jab, knuckles
become naughty, sore knockers
as she slow strolls her rooms

where she manages
to mash all the sharp notes

Low table corners,
desk chairs refusing to seat her,
a toilet lid with snapping mouth,
a fingernail idly scratching a small itch

Her once lovely, supple skin
now a mottling of tiny ruptures
pushing her life stream
outside normal boundaries

Now when did I do that, she points
and queries.
We smile and gaze, admire together
odd-shaped smears,
deep crimson bruising that blurs to yellow

Sometimes we give names,
like children
pointing out skin clouds

Lincoln in silhouette
in the center of her right calf,
this month's favorite

I calm my eyes
and determine these, too,
shall be absorbed, this surface suffering,

these pocks and pools of participation,
miniature sunsets adorning her aging canvas

OF GENERATIONS

EILEEN EARHART OLDAG

I am not old now, daughter, yet
all around me the horizon lifts
up by some power I never knew,
never suspected it had, it
lifts up a hard, vertical wall
that would be called Great, if
it were in China and I snapping

photos for an album before
turning my back, but everywhere
I see the horizon up before me
where there is no turning back,
nor am I first to face this
surface, sudden and untimely in
its rearing. I have teared its

unseen circumscription of my
mother and hers, not knowing
mothers further back, except
from photos in an album; I cursed,
grieved what it did to them,
what I suspected, what I knew it
could do to me, not even knowing

what it was. Now there is
relationship as I climb the
spiraled rungs of spines, scrub-
bent, child-weighted spines,
picking-cotton-sore spines of
mothers, spines prostrate,
circled up to stair above horizon—

263

lifted that I might have my due
perspective, that you might, too,
daughter, as you hear my spine
crack, as you will when you step
up on me. It is the promised
weight of your foot full on my
back that makes me know why my

mother smiled as she rearranged jars
saved in the cabinet over the stove,
makes me know why her
mother opened up seven times,
bearing for a daughter if it took
fourteen, makes me know that you
will want to grieve that I found

no door in this sepulcher of
generations, yet even now my
spine aches for your foot, to be
your hold, not as sacrifice or
duty, but as our rising, up, mutual,
your foot assuring that there is
order and that we are of it.

ONCE SHE FLOATS ON STONE

CHRISTY NOLAN

She was hardened by the scratch of Sunday;
through chain link to cemetery, stumbling silent
in parallel spirals while wind showered lilac on slate.

She'd only known grief in the context of life:
the purpose, the path. Then flood
washed courage clean from chest,
flushing soil she'd once matted flat.

Faith fell finite to fortune,
fable faded to fate, and loss rode tide
so high her home began to rot. What stood
sailed off so swift
she couldn't wish it well.

At once, she knew the sound of mourning
and all its waves and whirls.

She'd simulate sleep with prose and piano
while one dose, daily, before bed, shrunk
meaning microscopic.

No one grabbed a paddle
once she sank
to starting
over.

Alone, she learned to float,
then kick, then crawl
to open shore.

She used to swim
to strangers; someday
she will again.

YEARS LATER I STILL REMEMBER THE DAY

MELODY WANG

I swam at Swami's Beach with someone I had called
    a friend, late-day sun on our shoulders, fever-dream
        warmth of waves letting us forget the demanding
  world

when I was caught in a sudden undercurrent, floundering
    body flung into another realm — a rag doll swept into
nature's
        seemingly endless tilt-a-whirl, all sense of time
    and orientation

ripped from me: variations of the girl I had once been, from
    a luminous era when life was an apple-cheeked darling to
hold and give
        back to eager arms instead of a rusted ice cream
    machine that only dispensed

the briny taste of loss. Underwater, I was out of my body and saw
    myself: a raven-haired woman in a vintage summer dress,
unaware
        she was drowning, who laughed to mute pain,
    slim neck thrown back

as an offering to the sea & the loyal way it kept secrets—fully formed,
miniature
    versions of her discarded self, bloom-suspended around
her, skittish. Saltwater-
        preserved creatures with patient faces plump
    with possibility who waited for her

to realize that all that had bound her for so long she could now cradle in
arms
    that had once hugged cold tile after each absence. Silent
buoys, these tiny

soft creatures lifted her body to give her the
chance they always sought

to flourish: *begin by letting go*   this mantra
morphed into
              a lifeline that propelled me back into my body. I moved my
heavy limbs with
                            eager, horizontal strokes, guided toward a light
              I thought I'd never see again —

a salt-purged redemption I did not deserve. All around me, slow swirls
              of golden hues melded with the darkness of each memory I
tried to drown.
                            When I broke the water's surface, I gasped as I
              glided away from the gallows

that had engulfed me. I heard their watery voices murmur once more
              from the depths:

              we understand

why you had to   *let us go*

we forgive you   *now*

267

CONTRIBUTORS

Tiffiny Rose Allen is a reader, dreamer, craftsmen, and writer. She is in constant need of coffee to seize the day and books to ease her mind. Writing has always been her peace of mind and way of dealing with life. When she's not writing she's dabbling in creating jewelry, photographing nature, and petting her cats.

Anaum is a woman of conflict. Having spent most of her life in Kashmir, a UN designated disputed land, she has grown to see the worst victims of violence and war being women. She has worked quite closely with women near border areas to enlighten them about menstruation and the taboo surrounding it. She believes women don't have to be made strong because they are already strong and the world needs to get used to that strength.

Sloane Angelou is a storyteller & writer of West African origin; passionate about learning of human existence by interrogating human experiences. They exist in liminal spaces.

Amy Barnes has words at *FlashBack Fiction, McSweeney s, Popshot Quarterly, X-RAY Lit, The Molotov Cocktail, Lucent Dreaming, Anti-Heroin Chic, Flash Frog, Janus Literary, Perhappened, Cabinet of Heed, Spartan Lit* and many others. She's a *Fractured Lit* associate editor, *Gone Lawn* co-editor and reads for *Narratively, Retreat West, NFFD, CRAFT,* and *The MacGuffin.* Her work has been nominated for the Pushcart Prize, Best Microfiction, and longlisted for Wigleaf50. Her debut flash collection *Mother Figures* was published by *ELJ Editions* in June 2021. A full length collection is forthcoming from *word west press* in Spring 2022.

Wendy BooydeGraaff is the author of *Salad Pie*, a children's picture book published by *Chicago Review Press/Ripple Grove Press*. Her fiction, poems, and essays have been included in *NOON, South Florida Poetry Journal, The /tɛmz/ Review, The Dillydoun Review*, and elsewhere. Born and raised in Ontario, Canada, she now lives in Michigan, United States.

Ronda Piszk Broatch is the author of *Lake of Fallen Constellations*, (*MoonPath Press*). Ronda's current manuscript was a finalist with the Charles B. Wheeler Prize and Four Way Books Levis Prize. She is the recipient of an Artist Trust GAP Grant. Ronda's journal publications include *Blackbird, 2River, Sycamore Review, Missouri Review, Palette Poetry*, and *Public Radio KUOW s All Things Considered.*

Megan Cannella (she/they) is a Midwestern transplant currently living in Nevada. Her debut chapbook, *Confrontational Crotch and Other Real Housewives Musings*, is out now and available at https://linktr.ee/mcannella.You can find Megan on Twitter @megancannella.

Elizabeth M. Castillo is a British-Mauritian poet, writer, indie-press promoter. She lives in Paris with her family and two cats, where she writes a variety of different things under a variety of pen names. In her writing Elizabeth explores themes of race & ethnicity, motherhood, womanhood, language, love, loss and grief, and a touch of magical realism. She has words in, or upcoming in *Selcouth Station Press, Pollux Journal, Revista Purgante, Feral Poetry, Streetcake Magazine, Fevers of the Mind Press, Bandit Fiction, Epoch Press*, among others. Her bilingual, debut collection *Cajoncito: Poems on Love, Loss, y Otras Locuras* is available for purchase from her website/available on Amazon. Elizabeth's poem, "The Other Woman," was short-listed for Fresher Poetry Prize 2021 and published in their short list anthology. You can connect with her on Twitter and Instagram @EMCWritesPoetry.

Ellen Clayton is from Suffolk, England where she lives with her husband and three young children. She's recently been published in *Delicate Friend, Corporeal* and *Honeyfire*, amongst others. She has poems forthcoming in various publications including *Nightingale and Sparrow, Gutslut Press* and *Cauldron Anthology*. Her poetry can be found on Instagram @ellen_writes_poems and she's on Twitter @el_clayton.

Kai Coggin (she/her) is the author of four poetry collections, most recently *Mining For Stardust* (*FlowerSong Press* 2021) and *Incandescent* (*Sibling Rivalry Press* 2019). She is a queer woman of color who thinks Black Lives Matter, a teaching artist in poetry with the Arkansas Arts Council, and the host of the longest running consecutive weekly open mic series in the country— Wednesday Night Poetry. Recently awarded the 2021 Governor's Arts Award and named "Best Poet in Arkansas" by the Arkansas Times, her fierce and powerful poetry has been nominated four times for The Pushcart Prize, as well as Bettering American Poetry 2015, and Best of the Net 2016 and 2018. Her poems have appeared or are forthcoming in *POETRY, Cultural Weekly,*

SOLSTICE, Bellevue Literary Review, TAB, Entropy, SWWIM, Split This Rock, Sinister Wisdom, Lavender Review, Luna Luna, Blue Heron Review, Tupelo Press, West Trestle Review, and elsewhere. Coggin is Associate Editor at *The Rise Up Review*. She lives with her wife and their two adorable dogs in the valley of a small mountain in Hot Springs National Park, Arkansas.

Betty J. Cotter is the author of the novels *Roberta's Woods* (Five Star, 2008) and *The Winters* (which earned her a Fiction Fellowship from the R.I. State Council on the Arts). The first chapter of her novel, *Moonshine Swamp*, was selected for the premiere issue of *Novel Slices* (2020) and nominated for a Pushcart Prize. A Rhode Island resident, she holds an MFA in writing from the Vermont College of Fine Arts.

Rebecca Cuthbert lives, writes, and reads in Western New York. Her work has appeared in *Brevity, Slipstream, Neworld Review, Blueline Magazine*, and elsewhere. Her story, "Joiner," placed as a finalist in the 2021 New Millennium Writing Awards. She serves as managing editor for *Leapfrog Press* (leapfrogpress.com), and is currently working on a story collection.

Pam R. Johnson Davis is an award-winning poet, author, singer, songwriter, and historian. She loves to write poetry that explores life, love, and loss. You can find her poems in *Ghost Heart Lit Mag, The Bitchin' Kitsch, Mental Realness Mag, TunaFish Journal, Oyster River Pages, Square Wheel Press, Tether's End*, and *Pages Penned in Pandemic*. Her first poetry manuscript, *Seasons (I'll Be Seeing You): A collection of poems about heartbreak, healing, and redemption* can be found on Amazon.

Kiri DeLandé is a black, queer poet from New England. When she's not writing, she loves baking bread, lighting candles, and admiring the moon. Her most recent words can be found in *Ink Drinkers Magazine*.

Laura Dobson lives in London with twenty-four houseplants. She writes to navigate difficult moments and relishes sharing the therapeutic potential of creativity with young people. She has recent work with *The Phare Literary Magazine* and *Retreat West* and tweets at @laurarose_13.

Abigail Eckstine (they/she) is a 25-year-old queer writer of novels and poetry, parent-to-be and the founder of *Cauldron Anthology*. Most recently they have been published in Catatonic Daughters and Alternate Route. You can find them on twitter @whimsywriter3.

Ashley Marie Egan is an American poet, writer, photographer, and artist. Her work touches on themes of love, grief, trauma, feminism, mental illness, and all the joys and perils of life. She is the author of poetry and art collection *The Elements Between Us*. Her work has been featured in *Thought Catalog*, *Harness Magazine, Hey Ponderer*, and published in the anthologies *Mosaic: A Collection of the Instagram Poetry Community* and *Neverlasting: Poetry of Love, Lust & Lechery*. When she is not writing or working on her art, she is running a small business with her mother and little sister or spending time with her herd of dogs and cats. You can find her on Instagram @ashleymarieegan.

Suzy Eynon is from Arizona and lives in Seattle where she works in college admissions. She has a BA in English Literature and a certificate in literary fiction from University of Washington, and an MEd in Adult Education from City University of Seattle. Her fiction and poetry are published in *Overheard Lit, Hungry Ghost Magazine, Daily Drunk, Sledgehammer Lit, King Ludd's Rag*, and others.

Laci Felker lives in Baton Rouge, Louisiana, with her partner and their two cats. She just received her Bachelor's in English with a minor in history from LSU and recently began working at a local magazine. She enjoys reading and writing in her spare time, but she's still trying to find her voice. She has one previously published poem in *Openwork Magazine* called "Unfamiliar."

Mariana Feyt is a 25-year-old medievalist, poet, and frustrated Brazilian who has found in poetry the means to give voice to the earnings of her heart. She has a Bachelor's in English from the University of the State of Rio de Janeiro, where she's also pursuing her Master's in English literature. She can be found lurking on twitter at @Feyt_Mare.

Julia Figliotti (she/her) is a full-time writer and published author of short stories, poetry, and several books and articles on the science of creativity. With a BA in Writing from SUNY Buffalo State and an MSc in Creativity from the International Center for Studies in Creativity, Julia professionally dabbles in a range of fields outside of writing, including musical performance and voiceover work. Her passions lie in community- and heart-based activism, writing children's stories, and exploring the power of her own voice.

Caroljean Gavin's work is forthcoming in *Best Small Fictions 2021* and has appeared in places such as *Milk Candy Review, Barrelhouse*, and *Pithead Chapel*. She's the editor of *What I Thought of Ain't Funny*, an anthology of short fiction based on the jokes of Mitch Hedberg published by *Malarkey Books*. She's on Twitter @caroljeangavin.

271

Kyrah Gomes (she/her) is a queer poet and fresh fruit aficionado from NYC, currently living in Tampa, FL. Her poems have appeared in *LEVITATE, Journal of Erato, The B'K, warning lines mag*, and other publications. Her debut poetry collection, *sunlight for breakfast*, is available from *bottlecap press*.Uyou can send her comments, hate mail, or playlists on Twitter @reveri3s, or Instagram @kyrah.isabel.

Molly Greer was born and raised in the suburbs of Washington, DC. She currently resides in western Maryland with her husband and two children. Her work has appeared or is forthcoming in *34 Orchard, Green Ink Poetry, Last Leaves Magazine*, and *Sledgehammer Lit*. You can find her on Twitter: @MKGreerPoetry.

N. E. Griffin lives in Arlington, VA and works for the federal government. She is a lifelong writer and poet whose work has appeared in the *Constellate Literary Journal*, the *Dear Leader Tales* anthology, the *Pages Penned in Pandemic* print collective, and *Analogies & Allegories Literary Magazine*. You can follow her on Instagram and Twitter @n_e_griffin or on her website at www.negriffin.com.

Dr. Manjusha Hari is from Kerala, India and holds a PhD in Malayalam. She is really interested in reading and writing. She had been published in two solo poetry collections in malayalam and five anthologies as a co-author. She has published poems in national and international magazines.

Lindsey Heatherly is a Pushcart and Best of the Net nominated writer with work in *X-R-A-Y, Pithead Chapel, Emrys Journal Online* and more. She is the author of the poetry chapbook *Golden Hour Minus the Glow* (*Between Shadows Press*, 2021) and lives with her daughter in Upstate South Carolina. Find her online at https://r3dwillow.wixsite.com/rydanmardsey or on Twitter: @rydanmardsey.

Kris Hiles is an autistic lesbian creative. She lives in a New England dream with her wife, plants, and record collection. You can probably find her at a ballgame or museum, or on Twitter @KrisHiles.

Amanda Hurley is a New Zealand writer, editor and translator, currently based in East Germany. Her poems and short fiction have been selected for publication by *Cloud Ink, Flash Frontier, Flash Fiction Magazine, Globe Soup, Capsule Stories*, and *Red Penguin Books*.

Christiana Jasutan (she/her) is a Chinese-Indonesian writer currently pursuing her degree in BA English and Creative Writing at the University of Birmingham. She is the Publication Editor for *Writers Bloc* and an Anthology Editor for *small leaf press*. She explores the body, identity, childhood, love, emotions, and metaphors in her work. Chat with Christi on her Twitter @ChristiJasutan, or find more of her work on Instagram @cacaolatte.writes.

Teigan Jaymes has always called Utah home. While she finds comfort in familiar stories, getting to write her own felt more like cartography, mapping memories and wishes onto the page. Often disappearing into the woods with her dog, you won't find Teigan on social media.

JGeorge (she/her) currently writes from Pondicherry. Her poems appear or are forthcoming in Borderlands: Texas Poetry Review, West Trestle Review, Lumiere Review, Literary Shanghai, Mookychick and others.

Ai Jiang is a Chinese-Canadian writer and an immigrant from Fujian. She draws on cultures and landscapes of the lands she has walked for inspiration. Her work has appeared or is forthcoming in *The Dark, Prairie Fire, Hobart Pulp, The Dread Machine*, among others. Find her on Twitter (@AiJiang_) and online (http://aijiang.ca).

Thaina Joyce (she/her) is a Brazilian-American poet and educator based in Maryland. Her poetry has been featured at *Sledgehammer Lit, Olney Magazine, Lumiere*, and elsewhere. She hopes her work will empower, connect the human experience, and evoke new perspectives. Find her on Instagram: @thainawrites Twitter: @teedistrict.

Anita Kestin, M.D., M.P.H., is a physician who has worked in academics, nursing homes, hospices, public health, and the locked ward of a psychiatric facility. She is also the daughter (of immigrants fleeing the Holocaust), a wife, a mother, a grandmother, and a progressive activist. Although she has been writing for many years, she has only started to submit work (fiction, nonfiction, and poetry) during the pandemic. Her first non-scientific piece was accepted when she was 64 years old.

Aishwarya Khale has studied creative writing at Exeter college at University of Oxford. She is a volunteer at United Nations India and a member of Screenwriters Association (SWA), Mumbai. Her poetry has been published in *Mississippi Publishing Magazine*. Her short story, 'Farewell to the sea', has been published on Barnes and Noble and the Apple iBooks platform. Her travelogue has been published with *Tripoto India* and a poetry (open mic) was published with *Kommune India*.

273

Kayla King (she/her) is the author of *These Are the Women We Write About*, a micro-collection published by *The Poetry Annals*. She is the founder, Editor-in-Chief, and contributing writer for two collectives: *Pages Penned in Pandemic* and *The Elpis Pages*. Kayla's work has been nominated for a Pushcart Prize and made the Backlash Best Book Award shortlist. Her fiction and poetry has been published by *Fireworks Magazine, Sobotka Literary Magazine,* and *Capsule Stories*, among others. You can follow Kayla's writing journey over at her website: kaylakingbooks.com or her twitterings @KaylaMKing.

Margaret Koger (she/her) is a Lascaux Prize Finalist. A school media specialist with a writing habit, she lives near the river in Boise, Idaho. Her poetry adds new connections to the wayward web of life. See a few more poems at: *Amsterdam Quarterly, Collective Unrest, Inez, Voice of Eve, Headway,* and *Tiny Seeds Literary Journal*.

JoAnn Koozer is lucky enough to be part of a family of long-lived women who shared their lives with gusto.

Jasmina Kuenzli (she/her/hers) is an author of poetry, creative nonfiction, and fiction and has been published with *Small Leaf Press, Pidgeonholes, Defunkt,* and many others. She hopes to one day land a back flip and be a contributor on Drunk History. She would like to thank Brenna and Sarah, who hear all these stories first, and Harry Styles, who is sunshine distilled in a human being. Find her on Twitter @jasmina62442 and on Instagram @jasminawritespoetry.

Jasmin Lankford is a writer and world wanderer from Florida. She works in social media marketing and hosts a travel video series. In addition to Pushcart Prize and Best of the Net nominations, Jasmin's poetry has either appeared or is forthcoming in *Parentheses Journal, L'Éphémère Review* and elsewhere. Jasmin is in the process of publishing her debut poetry collection. She studied Creative Writing in France at the American University of Paris and graduated from the Zimmerman School of Advertising and Mass Communications at the University of South Florida. Find her on Instagram @jasmin_justlisten or visit her website at jasminlankford.com.

Holley Long is a storyteller based in Orlando, Florida. Currently she works in social media marketing, and when she isn't posting on Instagram, she's writing stories that make her heart sing or detailing her trials and tribulations as an aspiring author on her website awriterslifeforme.com.

Vanessa Maderer was a young reader turned editor, writer, and finally enthusiastic poet who has recently debuted her first chapbook entitled, *Cusp of Dusk* after a decade of revision. Now, she has an insatiable appetite for new ideas and themes, and can be found most easily through Twitter at @MadererV.

Abbie Madigan is the world's greatest pre-posthumous poet and beleaguered civil servant. Somewhere in the North of England. Of childbearing age. Unpublished—until now.

Annie Marhefka is a writer in Baltimore, Maryland. She delights in traveling, boating on the Chesapeake Bay, and hiking with her toddler. Her work has been featured or is forthcoming in *Coffee + Crumbs, The Phare, Capsule Stories, Cauldron Anthology, For Women Who Roar, Sledgehammer*, and *The Hallowzine*. Annie is working on a memoir about mother/daughter relationships; you can find her writing on Instagram @anniemarhefka, Twitter @charmcityannie, and at anniemarhefka.com.

Natalie Marino is a poet and physician. Her work appears in *Bitter Oleander, EcoTheo Review, Kissing Dynamite Poetry, Leon Literary Review, Midway Journal, Moria Online, Oyez Review, Shelia-Na-Gig online*, and elsewhere. She was named a finalist in Sweet Lit's 2021 poetry contest. Her micro-chapbook, *Attachment Theory*, was published by *Ghost City Press* in June 2021. She lives in California.

Anisha Mansuri is a poet, freelance journalist and editor. She writes on issues surrounding the experience of the South Asian diaspora, female beauty ideals and women in media and politics, through use of the mythical, magical, maddening and mundane. Having just finished her Masters in Creative Writing at the University of Birmingham, she is now working on her debut poetry collection titled *Homecoming*.

DW McKinney is a Black American writer living in Nevada. She serves as an associate editor for *Shenandoah Literary* and writes a graphic novels review column for *CNMN Magazine*. Her writing has appeared in publications like *Los Angeles Review of Books, Hippocampus Magazine, Narratively, PANK*, and the anthology *I'm Speaking Now* (Chicken Soup for the Soul, 2021). She is the recipient of a 2021 "My Time" Fellowship from the Writers' Colony at Dairy Hollow and a 2021 BIPOC Editorial Fellowship in Nonfiction from *Shenandoah Literary*. Say hello on Twitter @thedwmckinney or at dwmckinney.com.

Jennifer Mitchell is an emerging writer from Detroit, MI. Her poetry is forthcoming in *Moss Puppy Magazine*. She is working on her first sci-fi novel.

Zoë Morgan is a freelance writer based in Tbilisi, Georgia. She mainly makes a living writing film listicles, but pursues her literary ambitions in her free time. Her one virtue is her commitment to hydration, while her biggest vice is copious procrastination.

Christine Naprava is a writer from South Jersey. Her work has appeared or is forthcoming in *Contrary Magazine, Kissing Dynamite, Punk Noir Magazine, Literary Yard, The Daily Drunk, Outcast Press, Anti-Heroin Chic, the Lunch Break Zine, Sledgehammer Lit*, and *Rough Diamond Poetry Journal*, among others.

Rachel Nevergall shares her home in Minnesota with her husband and three children. She is the curator of family adventures, lover of all of the library books, mixer of fancy cocktails, and writer in the in-between. You can find her work on various publications such as *Coffee + Crumbs, Kindred Voice magazine*, and *Kindred Mom*, as a regular contributor for *Twin Cities Mom Collective*, and on her own website Rachelnevergall.com.

Christy Nolan (she/her) has always found comfort in the notes on her hand-me-down, cracked-up iPhone. Her story is nothing short of standard, though she found a strong voice in it, nonetheless. Christy's work in this collective charts both loss and discovery, and dreams of serving as a means to heal. "For Body, For Mind" was written Summer 2020 and first appeared in *Pages Penned in Pandemic*. "Once She Floats on Stone" was written Fall 2021 and is dedicated to South Shore and Bay Beach and the people who shared them with her.

Maria O'Brien is an Irish author of short stories, plays and novels. She studied English at Trinity College Dublin and draws her influences from all types of mediums, be they art, cinema, literature, or television. She is most happy when spending time with Hugo, her goofball Weimaraner.

Eileen Earhart Oldag was born and raised in Texas, like generations of women on both sides of her family, and she has long-lived in Southern states. She was a founding member of Upper Gladstone Writers 'Workspace in Shreveport, Louisiana. She now lives in Boise, Idaho, and is most recently published in *Writers in the Attic* anthology.

Stephanie Parent is a graduate of the Master of Professional Writing program at USC. Her poetry has been nominated for a Rhysling Award and Best of the Net.

Serena Piccoli (she\her) is a speechless charlatan who writes poems and plays about contemporary social issues and takes photos of nature and graffiti.

Jody Rae's work appears in *The Babel Tower Notice Board, The Avalon Literary Review, The Good Life Review*, and *Red Fez*. Her short story, "Beautiful Mother," was a finalist in the Phoebe Journal 2021 Spring Fiction Contest. She was the first prize winner of the 2019 Winning Writers Wergle Flomp Humor Poetry Contest for her poem, "Failure to Triangulate." She has pieces forthcoming in *Sledgehammer Lit, RESURRECTION magazine*, and *X-R-A-Y Literary Magazine*. Her work can be found at www.criminysakesalive.com.

Crystal Rowe is a former real estate attorney born and raised in Georgia, who now lives in small coastal town north of Boston. She adores the beach and would spend every waking moment there if she could. Crystal home educates her two daughters and spends whatever free time she can find writing, cooking, or reading. You can find more of her writing at SoulMunchies.com.

Beatriz Seelaender is a Brazilian author from São Paulo. Her fiction has appeared in *Cagibi, AZURE, Psychopomp*, among many others, and essays can be found at websites such as *The Collapsar* and *Sterling Clack Clack*, where she acts as Creative Nonfiction editor. Seelaender has only recently started submitting poetry, but her poems have been published by *Press Pause Press* and *The Graveyard Zine*. Her novellas, upcoming in 2022, have earned her both the Sandy Run and the Bottom Drawer Prizes.

Lindsay Stenico is a poet and fiction writer from Western Massachusetts. She graduated from Westfield State University with a BA in Communication and English. Her work can be found in *Dream Glow Magazine, Discretionary Love, Otherwords Press*, among other publications and forthcoming from *Penumbra Online*. She spends her time scrolling on Twitter as @lindsay_stenico, on Instagram as @dreamswitheyesopen, and on TikTok as @oopsanotherbooknerd. She also writes blog posts ranging from book reviews to thoughts on being a writer over on her website https://lindsaystenicoauthor.wordpress.com/.

Adrienne Stevenson is a Canadian living in Ottawa, Ontario. A retired forensic scientist, she writes poetry, fiction and creative non-fiction. When not writing, she tends a large garden. Her poetry has been widely published in print and online journals and anthologies, most recently in *Planisphere Q, Black Bough Poetry, MacroMicroCosm, Page & Spine, Poetry and Covid, Jaden, Still Point Arts Quarterly.* Her stories have won prizes in several competitions. Two have been published in Byline You can find her on Twitter @ajs4t.

Tessa Swackhammer is an emerging writer hailing from little Southern Ontario, where she grew up on a beach and learned to hate the smell of fish. Her work has been featured in publications like *Jaden Magazine* and *City Limits Press*, as well as being shortlisted for the *Plough Arts Prize for Poetry* (2021) and a current standing on the long-list for the Fractured Literary Flash Fiction Prize (2021).

Nicole Tallman is the Poetry Ambassador for Miami-Dade County, Associate Editor for *South Florida Poetry Journal* and Interviews Editor for *The Blue Mountain Review*. Her debut chapbook, *Something Kindred*, is forthcoming from *Southern Collective Experience Press*. Find her poems in *Wrongdoing and trampset*. Find her on Instagram and Twitter @natallman.

Elyssa Tappero is a queer pagan who writes fragments of prose and poetry about mental illness, paganism and witchcraft, queerness, and how it feels to be alive for the end of the world (which is pretty not great) in hopes of touching others who might feel the same. You can find more of her work at www.onlyfragments.com and follow her on Twitter at @OnlyFragments.

Stephanie Kadel Taras has authored multiple books in twenty years as a freelance writer in Ann Arbor, Michigan, including the award-winning college history *On Solid Rock* and memoir *Mountain Girls*. Her work has also been published in *Bear River Review, Belle Journal, Yellow Arrow Journal, Pages Penned in Pandemic, Second Chance, Detour Ahead*, and the *Ann Arbor Observer*.

Claire Taylor is a writer in Baltimore, Maryland. Her work has appeared in a variety of publications. She is the author of a children's literature collection, *Little Thoughts*, as well as two micro-chapbooks: *A History of Rats* (*Ghost City Press*, 2021) and *As Long as We Got Each Other* (*ELJ Editions*, 2022). Claire is the editor in chief of *Little Thoughts Press*, a print magazine of writing for and by kids, and serves as a reader for *Capsule Stories*. You can find Claire online at clairemtaylor.com and Twitter @ClaireM_Taylor.

Maria Uriarte Torrontegui was born in Chita, Russia, the 23rd of April of 1999. Since 2008, she has lived in Spain. Today, she is a medicine student at the University of the Basque Country. Maria has appeared in an Ararteko campaign for equal rights between men and women and has been a bit player in the Alardea TV show, directed by David P. Sañudo. Her first publication is included in the *The Elpis Pages* magazine.

Brittney Uecker (she/her) is a librarian, writer, and mother living in rural Montana. As a true Scorpio, she is drawn to the dark underbelly of everything and strives to reveal it to the world through her fiction and poetry. Her work has been published by *HAD, Taco Bell Quarterly, Fever Dream Magazine*, and others and she is a Best of the Net nominee for fiction. She is @bonesandbeer on Twitter and Instagram.

Melody Wang currently resides in sunny Southern California with her dear husband. In her free time, she dabbles in piano composition and also enjoys hiking, baking, and playing with her dogs. She is a reader for *Sledgehammer Lit* and can be found on Twitter @MelodyOfMusings.

Lizzie Wann was an integral part of the development of the San Diego poetry scene in the late 90s and early 2000s. She helped bring slam poetry to the city and produced original shows that featured poets and musicians. She hosted readings at venues across the city including Java Joe's, Urban Grind, Claire de Lune, and the Grassroots Oasis. She also founded and hosted the Meeting Grace house concert series that ran from 2000-2008. Her work appears on CDs (*A Wing & A Prayer and A New Leaf*), in chapbooks including *Familiars, Naked Wrists, and Complicated Skies* and in anthologies including *Comstock Review, Incidental Buildings & Accidental Beauty, A Year in Ink, So Luminous the Wildflowers, Don t Blame the Ugly Mug*, and *The San Diego Poetry Annual*. In 2019, her first poetry collection, *The Hospice Bubble & Other Devastating Affirmations,* was published by *Puna Press.*

ABOUT THE COLLECTIVE

The Elpis Pages celebrates fierce women, broken women, women of all shapes and sizes and colors and ages. Whether it be a howl or whisper, these women are using their voices however they can.

Sometimes all we have is hope.

All earnings from the print collective will be donated to the *Planned Parenthood Action Fund,* an organization which helps protect access to safe, legal abortion and reproductive rights.

To learn more, visit the collective page at kaylakingbooks.com or follow us on Twitter @TheElpisPages and Instagram @theelpispages.

Printed in Great Britain
by Amazon

18464593R10161